This book is dedicated to
Barros and t

The Brain Surgery Diaries: Journey from the Head to the Heart

It is my intention that this book will reach all of those it is meant to reach and together we will create a web of change around the world.

'Listen girl, I know you are a Psychologist and everything and you think you can heal people and rationalise their troubles away but GET OUT OF YOUR HEAD! Get out of your head and into your HEART and start Living!!'

After hearing this inner voice, Wendy decided to postpone death and become immortal...Because after all, living she wasn't. She was functioning in society and for her; death would have been a preferred option rather than simply existing by functioning. She was willing to explore the grey area between these two extreme polarities. And wow what an adventure this would turn out to be...

Introduction

This is an e-book about transformation which integrates psychology and spirituality in my own way. All I know is my own way following a difficult experience which turned out to be a real blessing. As kids, we believe in magic. Hopefully this book will reawaken a part of you which may lie dormant, or which has been lost and forgotten. Perhaps this book will assist you in connecting even more deeply with your inner child.

Hopefully this book will lead you to see the magic again in your own life and to remember how you don't have to be limited by your five senses anymore. I use humour throughout this e-book to remind both the reader and myself that life, including brain surgery and any other apparent traumas, can be perceived from a higher perspective as one big joke and to encourage you to embrace this perspective and to flow with this cosmic giggle. It doesn't have to be serious at all unless you choose to take this seriously, and where is the fun in that?

This e-book narrates my journey the only way I know how, via a stream of consciousness. I invite you to bear with me with my interpretation as well as to make your own. There may be some grammatical errors or mistakes although I try and avoid them, but I have already written my doctorate thesis so I am allowing myself to flow out of the confines of academia and be creative with language whenever I can. The only requirement is to keep an open mind so that you can see beyond these words and beyond your comfort zone, beyond the five senses, and start remembering what was never lost but lies dormant within the confines of our minds. The magic in this society hasn't been lost but it lies dormant within layers and layers of fear, indoctrination, pain, junk food, alcohol, drugs, caffeine, negative thought patterns and rubbish talk. Who gives me the authority to state all these things? Well I have given myself the permission to connect and know my own truth and I encourage you to give yourself the permission to think outside of the box too. Outside of the box is not a concept but a way of being which requires persistence and commitment. It takes trial and error to change an ingrained habit; it doesn't require you to have your head cracked open and stapled back together, although I know a lot of people who have lived through worse.

Let's start stripping off the layers, shall we? However, it is in your heart not your head that you will reconnect with the truth. This is one of the main things brain surgery has taught me and like I said, I don't recommend brain surgery to get to where I am at. All you need to do is to get to where you are at and believe your own truth by stripping off the layers of false thought that surrounds each and every one of us. If you weren't ready to perceive beyond the veil to believe the truth, and I am not saying there is one single truth to be grasped, well you wouldn't really be reading these pages. Maybe you are curious about me. I assure you that by taking this journey with me you will know that there is an easy way to be and be reminded of how beautiful life can transform in the depth of apparent human suffering. Thank you for being curious and open minded. Thank you for opening your heart to psychology and spirituality. Thank you for being ready to remember your own truth. Thank you to everyone who has assisted me in my evolutionary journey on Earth. Especially to those who told me a lot of negative things about myself and as a result made me connect to a resilience and strength within the depth of my Being which I would have never believed possible if you hadn't told me I couldn't do it. To all of those who rebelled in order to prove someone else wrong, I salute you.

A very brief introduction to me

If I think about my primary subjects, counselling and psychotherapy, let me start by being transparent. After several years of training, I started working for the National Health Service (NHS) in London in 2008. I was so disconnected, even after twelve years of training as a Psychologist, six years of seeing clients and having six years of personal therapy as part of my training. Then I found myself in 2010 working with over 26 patients in a busy primary care service, having a very short lived fling with one of my male colleagues who had a girlfriend at the time, and taking (very occasionally) recreational drugs. I was all over the place, but because I thought I was helping people and getting paid for it I thought I was doing well. I had a job, I had a title, I had prospects, I was finishing a doctorate, I had both a lot of responsibility and none. Truth is, spiritually I was a mess; but I kept the pretence pretty well together. I had friends who I could connect with on a superficial level but truthfully; my life, my job, my friends and all the places I frequented were devoid of any actual meaning. Scratch the surface and you will find nothing real. It was all a veneer.

At the same time, I could catch glimpses of connection between myself and my clients and that would make me feel better, sometimes. I was empty but I did not want to face the emptiness, looking instead for the next relationship and wine on the weekends that would frame a life with little content and a lot of text-book knowledge. I know that a lot of people might be able to connect to this meaninglessness; it overrides the daily noise like a soundtrack you can't get rid of.

My life had no heart, no spirit and no light. Therefore it didn't last very long. First I didn't stay in the job I was at and changed hospitals. At this stage my life had already started spinning. I mean literally spinning because the world would spin whenever I turned my head. It took me a year to get to the bottom of the spinning after I was misdiagnosed by my GP as having *'labyrinthitis.'*

Before that, therapy had only taken me so far as to gain enough self-respect to know that I didn't need to frequent horrible rock bars or chase after rock stars anymore. I was 23 years old when I first arrived in London, and it was then my wish to help people kicked in. First I had to save myself. If I fast forward to the period after my brain surgery I need to say that psychology no longer answered all the life questions for me. I wanted answers. I didn't believe the sayings*: 'Life is a lottery', 'There is no ghost in the machine', 'You were unwell and then you got better'* anymore. Those ways of attributing meaning were too simplistic for me. When something seemingly comes out nowhere and hits you sideways you start to look for other means of answering life's problems. On the other hand, I have trained as a psychologist since 2000, and I have worked as a counsellor and psychotherapist since 2006. So I know a lot about people, I know a lot about resistance to change and I know about overcoming resistance to change. I hope to share some of this knowledge on these pages as this e-book unfolds.

Finally, I am not teaching anyone how to live their lives. I am simply narrating my experience hoping my story can inspire you. There is no better time than now. Although I will use humour throughout the story because it is really quite funny, I can assure you that everything that I am writing about is based on fact. It really happened. I will be as honest and transparent about all the multifaceted ways in which we can explore the human experience because this is only one point of view. There is no better time than now so please get on board with me.

A dear spiritual teacher told me the first time we met: *'If you really loved yourself you wouldn't be doing the job you are doing now.'* Was she right? I think that the main problem with most people these days is that they really don't love, or even like themselves. All the issues I am encountering in my private practice at the moment boil down to this simple fact. Really, I was only starting to love myself when I started healing in this journey after my surgery.

There is always another layer and another layer of loving yourself that you can conquer. Most people I see in private practice don't even know who they are. If you can look at yourself in the mirror in those empty moments and feel at peace, feel tranquillity and feel that you fully love and accept yourself then congratulations you are already half way there.

I don't mean to be patronising here because for me, this is still a practicing exercise and it takes me to fall off the wagon sometimes to remember how it felt before I chose happiness again and again. I choose happiness; I choose love and choose the path of least resistance on a daily basis now. The Universe wants you to succeed, remember that and notice how much easier life becomes once you let go of the need to control the outcome of situations. Would you rather be happy or would you rather be right? You would be surprised at how many people choose the latter response again and again and again.

Before we get started, I want to reiterate something I learned in my continuous search for answers following my fall from academia. My fall from academia should be understood as my disillusionment that I could not find meaty (coming from a raw vegan in transition) answers to life's dilemmas. My fall from academia is the understanding that even if I had a PhD by the time I was 30 years old; it would all ultimately be meaningless. This would not suddenly give me a sense of respect and self-worth that I was seeking through academia. I had to do the inner work in order to connect with my self-worth. Self-worth is inherent and independent of what you do. Without further ado, I want to share a point by Leija Turunen, an energetic healer and health consultant. She made the following comment in one of her YouTube videos concerning an attitude of gratitude and expansion. She says:

Get a piece of paper and write;

Archangel Michael (if you don't believe in angels, just write, "Dear God" or "Dear Universe" or whatever works for you).

What do I need to release to be fully on my path and purpose?"

Try this now, let it flow. You are free to contemplate for a moment what it would be like to be in alignment with your higher-self, your true passion and your true purpose. What it would be like if you didn't feel the need to follow the rules, to pay the bills, to do this or that job that gives your soul no fulfilment. Let's try allowing ourselves to be free in our minds for a moment before the ego kicks in and justifies why you still need to put yourself into that glass cage. Really, the cage is open...

The cage has always been open. You did not come here to suffer. You do not need to do a job you hate and I know it's difficult to think outside of your own self-imposed restraints right now so please bear with me. For those who are reading this who are already activated and awakened, remember what it was like when you believed the illusion and how funny it is when you cease to limit yourself. Life is filled with love and possibility. If you choose to stay in your ego I respect and honour your decision too. Not all of us are prepared to give up everything familiar and gamble with fate. Not everyone is prepared to have no identity, to close your eyes and take that leap of faith off the cliff and into the void.

Into an unknown world off we go...

Prologue

Everything you need is inside you. Everything you want is already yours. Everything is possible and all the love you need is inside you now. You don't need to think about this. This is more of a feeling-level shift. If it weren't possible then you would not be able to imagine it. It is a miracle that I am here. It is also a miracle for you to be here at this point in time. We have both chosen to be on Earth at this time for a very specific purpose; to learn, develop, transform, manifest and inspire others to do the same. In order to inspire I need to share my story because only authentic stories will resonate on a human level. I feel that one of my purposes now is to follow my passion and to show you how you too can do the same. I know many people who are working a nine to five in a stressful job and even though they have money they are not ultimately happy. These people create dramas and relationships to give them a sense of purpose. I have been there, perhaps you have been too. This is ok. It is ok to be where you are at because the only way is up. I feel that you need to accept where you are at before we think about how to improve it. I talk about self-improvement not to conceal feelings of 'self-lack'. Because if you think you are lacking, how can you improve?

+ "The only way is up again"
Clean Bandit "Up Again"

13

I have always been an impatient person; I have always wanted to run before I could walk. This would come in handy when it came to getting out of a high dependency unit, or healing quickly. The day after I got out of hospital following major surgery I thought I would go upstairs to have a cup of coffee and I fainted in the bathroom. I was never one of those people who could simply put their feet up and allow themselves to be looked after. As soon as I had all the catheters out I was walking around the place carrying a bag which drained fluid from my brain; even securing it on metal bars in the bathroom in order to have a shower. I will get to this stage. Allow myself to take you on my journey and I am sure some aspects might resonate with you. Other aspects might shift your perception slightly or you will learn something new about the world. There is nothing special about me and I know that we must all face tragedy at some point in our lives.

As an existential counselling psychologist and psychotherapist I see a lot of clients in my private practice who are suffering. They ask for immediate relief from their pain, without wanting to go into it or feel it. Pain can only transmute and transform once you fully experience it. I know this because I spent most of my existence, up until less than a year ago, trying to look for answers outside my body and outside of myself. I would overanalyze, rationalize, and create dramas and relationships to distract me from myself. It took brain surgery for me to literally stop and reconnect to a greater power.

Life can be magical and you can wake up each day feeling excited about what miracles and blessings life has in store for you. This will show you how you can create abundance in every area of your life: financial, work, relationships, love. I can show you this because I am on the same journey. I have suffered and struggled and eventually I came to choose love. I had no choice but to surrender to a power greater than myself. The key is to surrender and trust that the Universe will take you to where you need to go. A year ago I was told: *'Either you have brain surgery or you will die in six months to a year.'* I could have tried to control the outcome of this. Controlling the outcome would have made it so much more painful. Life is beautiful when you chose love and happiness on a daily basis. The ego will try to spiral you back into fear and pain so it takes commitment.

Finally, before we talk about passion and connection in the next chapters I need to tell you how I came to this place in my life.

The idea for this book came about during a Virgo Full Moon meditation at the Alchemy (a holistic yoga and meditation centre) in London's Camden Town on the 8th March 2012. Coincidence or not, that was exactly a year after my discharge

↦ I met Seb 08/06/14

from hospital following brain surgery. I was in a very different place back then. On some level, I know now that I had chosen to go through this experience, but what for? Well, brain surgery is what took me to where I needed to get to as quickly as possible. I needed to be here and I needed to share this story of surrendering in all its painful and raw details.

How can this story resonate with others to inspire people to connect with their passion? It does not have to be brain surgery to help you connect with your heart but in my case that is what it took. Please take this journey with me while I time travel to brain surgery and back into a more authentic and meaningful existence of reconnection with Source. Life spent running away from emotions in favour of mind and thought meant that my head literally had to be opened up. When it was, the doctors took something out which was seven centimetres in diameter and six months away from costing me my life. This made me revaluate my way of being. Living being guided by my emotions is much more fun. I can now, two months into my meditation practice, shift my own negative emotional states fairly easily. Even when facing more appointments, check-ups and MRI scans as I am now, I will regard this as an opportunity to stay present. I will process and release my fears. I might emotionally crumble for a few minutes or hours, or I might get angry. I don't know. In any case, I trust that I am the one who can lead me through this, who will make me show up for the life-assignments and release the fear and the story I no longer need. This story is only important as far as it allows you to connect with yourself further, to shift and process your own story towards a more meaningful life. As Katie Byron writes: *'who would you be without your story?'* The 3D, dense reality got boring after a while and I wanted more from life.

Firstly, let's go back to the day when I had the idea for this book. Before the meditation, I am standing on the platform at Camden Town station in London, feeling a little overwhelmed by collective emotions. Without thinking, I shake my neck a little and envision my imaginary wings stretching out. The tension in my back softens and I glance around. I am back feeling centred. I catch a stranger's eyes and feel that he intuitively senses a shift in the atmosphere. Of course, it could be my imagination. I am happy in this space of zero gravity. Everything is possible. For a moment time freezes. Then I feel separate again. My ego has tricked me that the stranger is following me and I identify with this illusion. I did a lot of work on myself following the aftermath of the operation. I was desperate to know whether it was all a big cosmic joke or a punishment. I worked with an amazing spiritual healer who helped me to let go of a lot of anger which I had towards my body and myself. As the anger - symbolized by the colour red - travelled down my body and was released, I had a feeling of expanding my imaginary wings for the first time. Whatever force or forces inspired me to surrender and travelled through surgery and recovery with me are still inspiring me to this day. I am very thankful to this collective and to all my human angels on Earth who came at exactly the right time when I needed them. They know who they are.

I kept a blog from the moment I found out about the surgery until I recovered. The chapters that follow are excerpts from this blog in its real, unedited, authentic content. At the end I will expand on how the whole experience has affected and transformed my life for the better.

I tell people that I haven't changed much since my brain surgery. This is a lie. It has changed me deeply and it continues to change me up to this day. Part of me died. I was forced to evolve. I am getting rid of old beliefs, behaviours and lifestyles that are no longer a part of me. I see people and I see love more clearly than ever. It shifted through and it made me see my parents and my brother as more human. They are not always perfect, no one is. But I forgive the past and I admire their strength and the love they have for me. I love them even more deeply because I saw and was touched by their helplessness and their humanity.

Another way in which my life has drastically changed is that it has become all about perspective. It was a solitary journey. One in which I felt deeply alone at times. In my loneliness I connected further with myself and with others.

Life is all about perspective. For instance, because I was in the MRI machine being injected with contrast a year after my operation I realised that I had some more healing to do. After the tests I got the results back for an important piece of work. The results no longer held the significance that they would have under 'normal' circumstances. Given that I spent the morning inside the MRI machine, a 60% on part of my doctorate research was no big deal. Life is about perspective when you need to learn how to surrender. If I did not surrender again in my follow ups, I am sure the contrast and the excruciating phase of waiting for the results would have been a lot harder. As I was called to evolve my consciousness through this experience I had to accept the not-knowing. I had to accept how small and insignificant my ego's attempt to control the outcome was. I had to accept that something bigger than me, working through me, was co-creating this experience. I could choose to see it as an opportunity for birth and growth or from the perspective of a victim of trauma.

I looked at myself in the mirror a year on from the operation. It was just after the follow up and the veins around my chest stood out like something out of X-Men. I blamed it on the contrast injection. How interesting and resilient the human body can be! Right after the operation, a year ago, I was desperate for answers. I started doing a lot of work on myself and initiated my own spiritual journey. I saw famous spiritual teachers. My life transformed as I consumed a lot of spiritual books. I remembered the purpose of my true nature and slowly woke up.

Walk with me on my journey from the moment I receive the news of the impending operation and my adjustments to it, to the present; the follow up and the spiritual journey I continue to undertake. The following chapters are my blog diary excerpts that were kept throughout my craniotomy. A craniotomy is when the doctors cut through the skull and access the brain before stapling your head back together. That is what it took for me to wake up and re-connect with my heart. I had overanalyzed my life away to the point of needing brain-surgery. It is worth here noting that the news of my diagnosis affected those close to me like a bomb going off in different directions; some ran, others ducked and yet others stepped forward. I will expand on the topic of intimate relationships in the next chapters. Surprisingly, someone I had only known for five months before my diagnosis became one of my biggest sources of support during my operation and its preceding months. I refer to him as my boyfriend (Jason) during the mid-chapters even though we are no longer a couple. We split up seven months after my operation and because I changed so much as a person, I feel I am no longer a vibrational match to that particular relationship.

Chapter 1- The joke is on me!

This part is an actual excerpt from my brain surgery diary which is very insightful, yet not very funny because at the time I was very scared. Although fear is ultimately an illusion, at the time I couldn't laugh about it: the joke was still on me. In order to preserve the authenticity of this e-book I thought I would keep the diary as it is; but I assure you if blood and gore is not your cup of tea, the book gets lighter again later on. If you would rather skip the needles and hospital beds you can go ahead to Part Four when a different perspective emerges. We all know what happens at the end of the operation anyway: I live! Otherwise, obviously, you would not be reading this right now...

Background - before the surgery

As a busy Counselling Psychologist working for the National Health Service in the United Kingdom, I believed that I was at the top of my game. I had status, responsibilities and a case load full of patients that I had to 'fix.' Therapeutic interventions had to be measurable and evidence based. In other words you had to produce results.

Given that the National Health Service (NHS) is a focus for the nation's anxieties, of course results were expected. However, more often than not the patient would get lost in therapeutic intervention. I believed in what I did but I burned out pretty quickly. I had to see over twenty five patients a week for short term therapy and fill out an online diary monitoring their anxiety and depression levels in order to justify the service's funding. Sometimes I would get tired and would forget a patient's name, or I would be staring at the clock wishing time would pass quickly. It was then that I was forced to encounter the National Health Service as a patient myself.

The symptoms first started in November 2010. I went to the gym, and as I lay down to stretch the whole room spun around and I felt sick. I remember very vividly how the girl next to me laughed, possibly thinking I looked quite funny... maybe I had worked out too hard? Maybe my dinner wasn't cooked properly? I was sick when I got home but didn't think much of it.

I was neglecting my body not only physically but emotionally as well. I was out of touch on every level. I believed I had eaten something wrong, so I didn't think much of my nausea.

The next day, loading up on coffee again to go to work, the room spun when I turned my head. I don't even remember when I went to the GP for the first time, except that it was when I got back from my holidays. The dizziness and spinning feeling when I turned my head fast would not go away. The GP was probably having a bad day when I first saw her and was quick to dismiss me as having 'labyrinthitis' and by giving me antibiotics.

This labyrinthitis, which is a common infection of the inner ear, seemed like a suitable diagnosis except that my symptoms were not getting any better. I would return to see her two more times complaining about my 'labyrinthitis'. She told me that labyrinthitis had no cure. I then told her that I could hear a rushing water noise in my right ear. The GP said that I should try *'listening to the radio'* to drown out this noise. Unconvinced, I eventually sought a second opinion. This is what saved my life. Certainly, I knew people who had labyrinthitis and had got better. At this point, there was no more silence in my head. I had to be very careful when turning my head quickly otherwise the whole room would spin around and I would feel that I would either be sick or faint. Funnily enough, there was only one head-ache. All this was before I even knew that my 'labyrinthitis' was a brain tumour.

In the end, there was a pulsating vein at the top of my left eye which I could see move with my heart-beats when I looked in the mirror. I had created a horror movie for myself, one which seemed completely out of control of and was only about to get worse, before it got better.

Diary entry 10th January 2011

The doctor said it was *'labyrinthitis'* again; it would *'come and go, there is no cure'* and gave me some medicine. I have seen the same unhelpful GP twice and complained about her saying it was *'labyrinthitis'* and wanting me to go away. I have never felt so angry at a doctor before. The second doctor I saw, in order to get a referral to see a physiotherapist, printed things off patient.co.uk and gave me medication which later transpired to be for *'Meunier's disease'*. I googled Meunier's disease when I got home and it looks as if Meunier's disease makes you go deaf in one ear. This would not be ideal given the job I do. He told me Meunier's disease and labyrinthitis are the same thing, but on paper they look very different! I am sure that in reality they feel different too as you go deaf if you have Meunier's disease!

At my parents' insistence I consulted with a private doctor about my 'labyrinthitis' symptoms that would not go away. I did not expect in my wildest dreams to find out what I have found out... I guess I am still digesting the facts. Firstly, the doctor I saw privately sent me to an ears-nose-throat specialist at Harley Street. This specialist asked for an MRI scan before he sent me to a physiotherapist who specialises in manoeuvres for labyrinthitis. He made me shake my head from side to side very fast and I felt very dizzy and nauseous when I tried that.

Upon my return he had my MRI scan on his display board. I will never forget this words: 'So... this is your brain, this (pointing at grey dark mass in the middle back of my brain) shouldn't be there... we don't know what this is, this is quite worrying...' I was very worried because apart from the dizziness that had persistently got worse over the whole year, I barely had any symptoms.

'What could it be doctor?' I asked. 'I am not sure, this is quite worrying as I wasn't expecting anything to show up on your scan. I will refer you to a neurosurgeon. I am speaking with him at two o'clock this afternoon. He will be in touch. His secretary will give you a call tomorrow. Have a good day. Bye.' was his response.

I left in shock. That image really struck me. What could that be? It was a grey dark mass in the middle of my brain. It was much bigger than both of my eye sockets combined. I cried all the way to the tube station and called my parents straight away. I thought I was going to die. The world changed colour, meaning and shape. A lot of thoughts went through my mind at this stage including: would I still be doing what I do now if I am going to die? My own response was no, I would want to be travelling the world, but I had no money to travel the world. We usually think the worst. Could it be cancer? I was convinced this was it. I was 29 years old and I had just been given a death sentence. Were my days numbered? Would I still be doing the work I do?

Then my mind went into denial; maybe they swapped the results. My brain was turning thousands of possibilities up in the air and I liked this last one best. This was nothing but a sick joke I had decided; they swapped the results. My parents on the other end of the line were incredibly calm: *'Don't be concerned about this, everything is going to be fine, imagine that thing in your brain getting smaller'* they reassured me. Then I decided to pretend this was not happening and went to get my hair done and meet a friend for a beer. She talked about the problems she was having with her boyfriend at the time and upon the revelation of my news she said: *'You need a miracle',* and carried on talking about herself. Looking back I cannot believe she was this insensitive. While most of my close friends panicked, others reacted in the opposite way. I don't believe there is a right or wrong way to react to bad news, and even when this experience cost me a lot of old friends, at the time I needed the distraction she provided.

The neurosurgeon called and wanted to see me the next day, Thursday 26th November at 2pm. I told his secretary I couldn't make it as I had client appointments that day. I then called my clients to cancel and headed over to a private hospital in London's St John's Wood. I was there at 12pm and my appointment was at 2pm. I just sat there facing the surgeon's room, waiting my turn. Once again, words I will never forget followed: *'So basically this is a cystic swelling in your brain, it is located in your cerebellum, which is a very primitive part of your brain and it could be affecting your balance.'*

My balance had started to be impacted by the tumour's growth. I had twisted my ankle twice and was not able to stand on one leg for long periods of time. I had seen a physiotherapist about this who gave me some simple exercises.

The neurosurgeon said I had a benign brain tumour and sent me for more tests. That afternoon in the MRI scanning machine I could watch the woman's face changing in the control room. She was being very friendly and sweet initially, and after she finished taking an x-ray of my brain she came in with a different expression on her face and said: *'I am not a doctor so I can't give you any results. Anyway, you know how well or not you are...'* Which of course I had absolutely no idea at that stage. She told me no news was good news and that the doctor would call me if it was something urgent. She also said that if I was her daughter she wouldn't want anyone who was not a doctor giving me any news. I could tell from her expression something was definitely very wrong. I wasn't consciously worried because I was in too much shock, I didn't cry. I was just getting on with my life... Then on the 8th December I had to get the results. My boyfriend at the time came with me.

Chapter 2- More scary health stuff

10th January 2011

I recently found out there is a cystic swelling or a benign tumour in my brain. It is precisely in my cerebellum. It has been there for a number of years and growing slowly. I have mentioned excerpts of my conversation with the doctors. They are all true. One NHS doctor told me to *'listen to the radio'* to drown out the water noise in my ear. She also got very annoyed with me and said there was *'no cure'*, that I had labyrinthitis and other misdiagnoses. I had complained about her but never received an answer. I should have gone and seen her when I had 32 staples at the back of my head, and asked her to remove the staples of my 'labyrinthitis'. As I write this now she no longer works at the practice following my complaint. I did not want a personal vendetta against this woman as I am sure she has her own problems. At the same time, I did not want her to be rude and dismissive to another patient in the future whom may need the same level of attention she was unable to give me. Certain things doctors said to me have helped to shock and humour me throughout this scary health stuff process. For instance, when I asked the doctor: *"Should I be worried doctor?"* His curt reply was: *"How can you not?"*

I went to see the neurosurgeon to get my result on 8th December 2010. My boyfriend insisted he would come with me and took the day off. Good job he did as I am sure I was there listening but I didn't hear a thing of what the doctor actually said. My boyfriend said he thinks I only heard about 20% of what the doctor said. This is another very interesting defence mechanism. I remember I just sat there thinking about my hair during the consultation.

I walked in there feeling scared and apprehensive. There was a huge image of my brain on the doctor's computer. In explaining my diagnosis, the neurosurgeon grabbed his plastic model of the brain which fell over and scattered its parts all over his desk. I remember thinking: *'Oh my gosh, if this is what he does to a plastic brain model what is going to happen to mine?'*

I looked at the image and felt numb. I remember feeling happy because my hair looked good. This was to not focus on the perceived emergency of the situation. I remember him saying bla bla bla cerebellar haemangioblastoma or pilocytic astrocytoma, migrated pushing against right ventricle... Could fill with fluid, shut down the right ventricle, as you can see... However, because nothing he was saying made any sense to me I asked him: *'So what's the worst that could happen doctor?'* *'Sudden death'* he answered.

Some people reading this might be familiar with this situation, most may not be. This was the last time I was ever to ask the: *"What's the worst that could happen"* question. The neurosurgeon talked about operating, which I didn't listen or hear and I told him I was going on holiday. I remember him saying we had three months to do something about it and I had to make a decision once I come back in January. I asked him whether I should do another MRI and he said only if I left it over three months. I left and went to collect my CD with the images of my brain from the Radiology Department. I felt numb. I went downstairs and got my CD and felt surprised that my boyfriend was crying. I remember that when the doctor said *'Sudden death'* I wasn't scared. At the time, I felt that this was no big deal as we are all going to die some day. Anyway, I felt that at least my death would be painless; I would be lying to say there was no appeal with regards to this imaginary escape.

Once I had a conversation with my ex-boyfriend about this and he said my denial was what he found most painful. At the time, I thought: *'I am taking my chances and not having the operation, I have no kids and I am ok to die. I am not leaving anything behind that I am responsible for except for my cat.'* This point of view has changed drastically now. Now, the surgery doesn't seem like that big a deal, but I will get to that part...

19th January 2011

I will start this one by saying that I did get a second and a third opinion in Brazil about my brain scan and they were even scarier than the first. It almost ruined my holiday. They made me feel like I was going to die and the sense of urgency that was not present with the doctor in London was amplified by the doctors in Brazil.

My cousin was very kind to get me the appointment with her friend, who is a neurosurgeon, and the guy who operates with him; and claimed he had 20 years of experience in the field. Part of my denial came from thinking that what they would say would differ and it wouldn't be as serious as what the neurosurgeon in London had told me. My cousin's friend started talking about an operation in which a catheter would be fitted, draining fluid from my brain indefinitely. That really freaked me out because Mr Bradford - my neurosurgeon here - hadn't mentioned that. Jason was a huge support to me because when I called him crying, paying loads of money for roaming, he assured me that the doctor here, who is one of the best in the world, said I had three months to do something about this. Mainly I listen but hear nothing about operations.

I went to Fernando de Noronha with my brother and my parents which is an amazing place, a paradisiacal island:

Heaven on Earth. The *Pousada* where we stayed was fantastic. We had a view of the blue sea and the beach and the rock, whose name I have forgotten now. I especially enjoyed walking by the seaside and getting my legs and feet stuck into the wet sand. There was a lot to do in Fernando de Noronha. Since I don't dive and Brazilian doctors told me I shouldn't, I went snorkelling at Praia do Sudeste and Atalaia and saw a shark, loads of sea turtles, millions of gorgeous colourful little aquarium fishes and an octopus. It is really a place worth visiting in your lifetime. Pousada Ze Maria has a food festival with 47 different dishes. I ate a lot. The only thing was that, following the doctor's opinion, I spent a while being hypersensitive and thinking I was going to have a convulsion and die... He said that if I faint it would be too late and I might have to undergo an emergency procedure. I spent a lot of time scanning my brain for every little subtle headache. I know that even when no one in my family would speak about this directly to me or share their worries with me, I could sense they were extremely worried. Apparently, as soon as we got to this place, my father went to check what the emergency procedures to leave the island were. This was because the Brazilian doctors wanted to pretty much 'sell us' a surgery and wanted to operate on me that same week, and keep me in hospital on the same day. My parents were very supportive during this meeting suggesting it was my choice. Yet, we decided to take the risk and go on holiday instead of staying in hospital. I would much rather die on the beach!

Then I had a dream while I was there and woke up without the water noise in my ear for a change. At this point I decided I wasn't going to die from this. However, the NHS has really let me down. I wrote them a letter this week regarding my misdiagnosis that could have cost my life. After Fernando de Noronha we went to Florianopolis and stayed in another amazing place by the sea. The sea in the south of Brazil is colder than in the North but I could actually get in and swim safely without being overpowered by six metre waves. There is always surfing at Fernando de Noronha and the water is crystal clear. I miss the food in both places already.

Chapter 3- Brain stuff

21st January 2011

I am almost thirty. These are my last four days of being a 29 year old. Without being over-dramatic, it is not a birthday I am looking forward to, and yet hopefully a time of healing and rebirth will emerge. I have begun telling my friends that I am having brain-surgery... one of my friends was telling me about her new job and date when she asked me: *'What's up with you?'* meaning job wise... *'Well, I am having brain surgery'.* I know it sounds bizarre. Seeing it in black and white in emails freaks me out. My colleagues and friends are surprised at how calm I seem about all this... Yesterday with the neurosurgeon it went better than I expected. I wasn't in denial, I didn't cry and he said the risks were minimal. When I asked him about a catheter he said: *'Yeah that could be a good idea'*- shouldn't he know? He will not perform the operation with me sitting down (unlike what they told me in Brazil, you don't operate on the brain while the patient is sitting down). It will last between three to four hours, and I will be in hospital for a week and need care for 15 days. It should take me one to three months to recover, according to him. My neurosurgeon is a rock-star, although I did not trust him initially he proved to be the best in his field. However, he is very skilled at never giving you a straight answer and: *'Perhaps'* or *'I will consider it'* were some of his most common responses.

This morning I woke up angry and upset... I think it takes me a while to deal with the stress of it. I went to work and saw the physiotherapist at the gym in the afternoon and I felt really let down by him. After promising a lot in terms of talking about it and a second opinion, he avoided me and never answered my email once I spelt the words 'cystic swelling' and 'operation'. Some friends, I feel, are writing my obituary: *'You have always been a strong, brave girl...'* A morbid part of me can't help but think this is what they would say in the event of my death. Hopefully that will not happen. Another friend was more helpful saying I should see this in terms of growth and healing and forget about my doctorate... I asked the neurosurgeon for another MRI scan and I will get the date for the surgery next week. I hope it is March because I want to postpone this as much as possible, or on the last day of February. Given that I live in London by myself, my parents need to fly over to be with me and are pressuring me for a date as they are worried. The thing that annoys me the most is having to have my hair partially shaved as they will have to access my cerebellum through the back of my head. This afternoon, I announced down the phone to my friend in a cafe that I am having brain surgery, and then to the hairdresser. The woman at the cafe just turned around and looked at me, and the hairdresser made some meaningless comments. It doesn't matter, and yet most emails are empty expressions of surprise from people, I don't think anyone knows how to react. People are used to operating like robots in their daily lives without any big news or changes. I think everyone struggles to cope with bad news: we don't like change. Hence empty reactions such as: *'This is my number, whatever you need'* are so devoid of understanding and feeling, they meant nothing to me. This evening I have decided to look on Amazon for books on brain surgery and will buy these two: *Brain Surgeon's Inspiring Encounters with Mortality* and *Surviving and Thriving Brain Tumour Survivors.*

But really, do I want to know what's inside my brain...? The doctor said it will hopefully be all over and done with after my operation.

Update 8th March 2012

In the end I bought Dr Keith Black's book on brain surgery and read it from beginning to end before my operation, becoming fascinated with all the case studies and what was to come. I was also comparing these patients with my own problem and felt relieved at how easy and simple my tumour seemed in comparison to what it could have been. I know this does not make any sense now, but with this information I felt less alone in dealing with my problem.

28th January 2011

Brain surgery is not a subject anyone wants to read about, unless they know someone who has had a stroke, a brain tumour or they are going through it themselves. I can't believe I am going through it myself! I have started reading 'Brain Surgeon' by Dr Keith Black and while I liked it at the beginning, now it just freaks me out, but on the other hand I am lucky that there will be no permanent visible scar (incorrect) and that it is a simple, straightforward procedure.

I have the date for the operation now so the countdown begins. I am using denial until I go in and get the angiogram, stay in hospital and have it done. Some stories inspire me; that it is not going to be so bad in the grand scheme of things. I don't want people to feel sorry for me and I don't want their fear. Emotions are contagious, especially fear. It's fine, it's painless and according to my boyfriend it might not be the worst thing that's ever happened to me. Child birth might be more painful, who knows. (Although now I feel I would take child birth any day over brain surgery.) I will feel no pain... In my mind I will be at the beach somewhere and I have enough resilience and support to cope with this. So let's hope for a speedy recovery.

I never hear anything the doctor tells me unless I ask him myself. In some ways I prefer him to the Brazilian doctors who freaked me out. I am not going to die from this I know that for sure. I want to get an angel tattooed on my neck but might that distract them during the procedure..? The doctor said to me today: *'I had a young guy, just like you with exactly the same thing, but then he had a haemorrhage before I had a chance to operate on him.'* *'What happened to him doctor?'* I asked. *'Oh... He died'* was his response.

Part of being between 'life and death' makes you feel more alive. I have no time for rubbernecking and people who just want to know for the pleasure of seeing someone else suffer. I know now who my true friends are and will earn my wings through this experience... As my clinical supervisor said: *'If it was easy then you wouldn't be earning your wings.'*

31st January 2011

This is a message for Dr Keith Black: Dear Dr Black, I have become aware of your work since I found out I have a cystic swelling in my cerebellum and started reading your book *Brain Surgeon*. I am a psychologist practicing in London and I realise that maybe you won't answer this email as I am not paying you millions of dollars for a consultation. However, I felt compelled to write. I am waiting for an operation on 5th March. The neurosurgeon that is doing it, Mr Robert Bradford, is doing an angiogram the day before. I guess he doesn't know yet whether it is a cerebellar haemangioblastoma or a pilocytic astrocytoma. (He knew.) I have no idea what the difference is and here they don't tell you much unless you bombard them with questions. I found out by accident as the national health system here kept telling me I had 'labyrinthitis' until I went to a private doctor and did an MRI scan. The only symptom I have is a pulsating water noise in my right ear which I am told could be my heartbeat as the pressure in my head is increased and is resonating with the fluid. I am lucky that I have no migraines or other symptoms; it was two years ago that I experienced some dizziness. Furthermore, I have been advised to go for the operation as my condition can cause further problems and sudden death. I believe that the area is easy to get to, and once removed I should have no further problems. Also recovery is likely to be fast. I understand that without seeing my MRI scan there is not much you can say but what got me thinking was chapter 4 in your book when you refuse to operate on someone with a cystic swelling on her brain stem and the part where you mentioned an astrocytoma. Can I trust the advice I have been given here in terms of a good prognosis and likelihood of 100% cure in this case? Thank you very much if you can find the time to reply to this email.

Update 8th March 2012

It is funny to look back and see how at this stage, I was bargaining and hoping for a miracle. Miracles did come eventually. However, Dr Black has not replied to the email above. On the other hand, my neurosurgeon knew exactly what he was doing.

Chapter 4- Emotions

The stage I was at one month before the operation and the different feelings I was experiencing were part of my day to day life. At this stage, I felt completely out of control with everything in my life.

1st February 2011

I am having real trouble controlling my emotions at the moment. I am usually a pretty levelled, stable person with very occasional ups or downs; but add PMS, a brain tumour and an operation date to the additional stress of doing my doctorate and all of a sudden I am all over the place. Yesterday for instance, I went to the gym; they played *'A Beautiful Day'* by U2. I don't really like that song but I almost cried... then I was happy because in my body I felt good, centred. Now the anger. Oh I just want to scream at someone and can see myself getting unusually irritated and wanting to shove people out of my way... It is not THEY who are annoying me but I am quite anxious and irritated in general... I keep imagining a huge horrible gash with stitches on the back of my head and a catheter poking out of the right side of my head and it really pisses me off. I know I should be happy, grateful for the healing; thanking God for my miracle etc but I just want to smash some plates, or cry, or do both! I understand what it must be like to want to eat until you are sick. I lose my appetite then get really hungry, then I feel sick. I need to give more love and learn how to be vulnerable and accept help... I need protection but I am sick of crying. I think: *'I don't want to see anyone',* then am angry, then I feel sorry for myself. At the moment this is constant. I am getting exceptionally annoyed when my boyfriend can't read my mind. I often think it would be easier if he wasn't around. Not that I don't want him around, he is lovely and supportive, but I get annoyed when he doesn't call me or accidentally walks away when I tell him I love him. It's silly. My emotions are all over the place. How much longer until I stabilize?

The pulsating heartbeat noise in my ear seems to be getting louder. Yes, this is due to the fact that the pressure in my head has increased and the blood pumping resonates with the fluid so I can constantly hear my heartbeat in my right ear. I almost don't know what it's like to wake up into silence, and I look forward to that. I can see a new vein behind my left eye and sometimes I can see it pumping to the same 'water' noise in my ear. It freaks me out; it's difficult to explain. It is like something out of a horror movie. Now, deep down I know that it will all work out in the end. I have to believe that. I need to find ways to minimize my suffering and stop being so angry and hateful. I need to use this experience wisely in order to embrace and mature through it, as opposed to acting out my fantasy of screaming at someone. If a client told me about hurting themselves or eating until they threw up, I would be able to empathize and say: *'It sounds to me like you are in so much emotional pain that you think hurting yourself in that way would make you feel better?'* Yes then why can't I do that for myself right now?

Chapter 5- I am ready

'Life will give you whatever experience is the most helpful for the evolution of your own consciousness.' Eckart Tolle

7th February 2011

The first dates the doctor gave me for the surgery were the 24th and 25th of February... I said yes initially but in spite of false bravado, I freaked out and backed out and asked for March instead. Now I have the dates for March. I washed my hair today after the gym and when I put my hair down to flick it back up with the towel I felt that weird dizzy sensation again... For a few seconds I was just thinking: *'Please God, Please God help me'* and hoping I wouldn't faint. Luckily, I didn't faint. The symptoms are getting worse; the noise in my right ear is getting louder, like a bee inside my head... I felt bad for making light hearted jokes of the situation and thought; this is a serious matter... I should not be laughing at the doctor's insensitive remarks about the guy with the same thing as I have who did not operate and died. At this stage I am ready. I am finally starting to feel 100% ready to embrace what lies ahead. I understand that I am lucky and I don't want to push my luck when I feel like the girl who has cheated death. I felt that I would have changed the operation dates to 24th and 25th if it wasn't for when my parents get here. I hope that things will stay fine and be fine until then. It is a serious matter and as much as I can tell myself, fool myself or think of myself as fine... this is happening and I have nothing else to do but to embrace it, gracefully. Imagining what will happen and the pain is silly. I like this feeling; the feeling of being above it and strong for it and indestructible, yet so vulnerable between life and death.

10th February 2011

Everything is going well and some random stranger chatted me up today. He said I looked 23 years old. This may be a line men use because they think it works with women. Obviously he has no idea that I am having brain surgery in less than a month. I am not sure what sort of energetic vibration might be emanating from me, yet I feel quite positive all things considered. I am off to the Mayfair bar for a drink with a friend. I have also started feeling a bit dizzy when I stand up quickly which can't be good, but it gives me a flavour of what is to come in recovery. At the moment I am happy, I can walk and do the cross-trainer without any problems. It is the little things that   keep   me   going.
I am quite attached to the little dramas of life. Like water and oil they don't mix with my experience; or they shouldn't, but

they do. I am keen and curious to find out what is going on in my friends' lives and their little dramas. Sometimes I feel more alive as if my self-awareness is being accelerated. Sometimes I feel very down like all of Tuesday evening and Wednesday. This is to do with feeling isolated in my experience, but I am always feeling something, and right now I feel really excited! One of the downers of my job is knowing when you are repeating patterns and barking up the wrong tree; but now I am liberated.

Chapter 6- Countdown to the operation

16th February 2011

This is what my brain looks like at the moment:

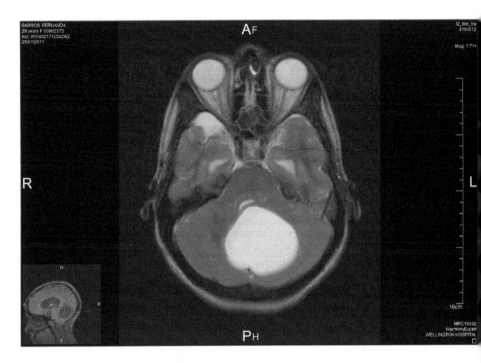

That big mass at the back should not be there. The other gray thing is the ventricle, that's ok to be there; obviously that little cyst at the back is what caused it but you can't see it from these images. The large area at the back of my head is the fluid. This 'thing' has been growing slowly for many years and my brain has adapted around it.

I have surgery in two weeks time. I feel a bit apprehensive... Up and down. It's difficult for me to relate to having this in my head because I am not getting any headaches. I am staying positive, I have to do my best, trust the doctor will do his best and surrender really. This is completely outside of my control. I can't wait until it is all over and I can get back to normal life. I feel that this will also make me a better psychologist as I will be able to empathize even more with life's difficulties and understand what someone in a similar situation might be going through. At times this can feel like a very isolating experience. Perhaps embracing and overcoming this challenge could be the best thing that's ever happened to me..?

21st February 2011

Eleven days until my operation. Just don't feel like I want to get out of bed at the moment, but I should save my apathy for when I really need it, post-op, as opposed to trying to guess what might happen after surgery: throwing up, insomnia, steroids etc? I am still working with clients at this point but I stop next week. It is difficult listening to clients when the noise inside my head is getting louder and louder, and it is very distracting. It is like my whole brain is pulsating, the sensation is hard to describe. I feel better when the noise subsides and yet this symptom is constantly present for me all the time. It looks like my cerebellum is squashed against the back of my head so the lack of symptoms surprises me. However, if I turn my head quickly sometimes in the middle of the night or lie down quickly with no support, that dizzy feeling comes up for a few seconds and it's like someone is squeezing my heart too. The squeezing heart is new and odd; I wonder whether it's apprehension? At the moment I am waiting until my parents get here and getting myself organized

Seven days

I feel like Donnie Darko - 60 hours, 93 seconds etc. But of course this is no psychological horror and the world is not going to end. It feels like a little death: it is. I have to go in, and I never had an operation before in my life, and then have brain surgery. It is all quite surreal.

A month ago I was saying: *'A month from now this will be happening'* and now it's a week. This time next week I will be in my hospital room waiting for brain surgery... and then its three or four days in ICU. Waiting is the worse, I hope that it is not going to be too bad and I know that everyone has a horror story to tell me at the moment about their own experiences with operations. This is not very helpful at all. The tips about asking for a sedative, to telling me in detail everything that can go wrong.

My parents got here this morning at 5am and I had to separate from my boyfriend, which was hard because I relied on him a lot for emotional support. I am very anxious today. Maybe running will make me feel better; but I am spending time with my parents. I feel like over eating but then I would just get fat; comfort eating but I would be sick. Last night I just felt sick. How can my cerebellum be squeezed so tightly at the back of my head yet I am presenting with no symptoms apart from the dizziness if I spin around quickly or throw my head upside down? How can the human body adapt to something the size of a fist inside your brain?

A lot of friends want to see me or speak with me which is nice but I feel like I haven't really got the time. Other people who seemingly didn't care because they are too wrapped up in their own problems really annoyed me. I forgive them because it is very hard even for me but a: *'How are you?'* would be nice. I mean, don't promise me loads of things; like my friend who is a nurse and asked me to call her. She said she would help me and give me loads of advice. I sent her an email with all the details because she works in the field; she cares for people who have had brain surgery. She didn't reply to the email, couldn't speak when I called and never called me back. This experience really made me see clearly who I want in my life and will choose to spend time with; and those who no longer serve my life's purpose and belong to a different lifetime. I was a different person before and parts of my former self are best left alone and buried.

I am the stereotypical Kubler-Ross person (Kubler-Ross wrote a model on the five stages of grief). I am up and down, up and down. I will call the nurse; yet I don't want people to know. I don't want the gossip to spread; especially to people that I went to university with. I don't want to be known as the girl who is 'having brain surgery'. I realise this is just a stream of thoughts but I feel better for writing it. Someone advised me not to forget to ask for a sedative before I go into the operating theatre because I don't want to be looking at all the machines awake, apparently... I will see. I will be stronger once this is over and everything is fine. Someday we can all learn from this. Besides, I am very lucky because if it is what I think and hope it is, my brain problem will be sorted once and for all and I will put it down to experience. I told Jason to scatter my ashes over the sea should I be the unlucky 1%. I don't think he liked that comment. Scattering my ashes over the sea in Australia or Brazil would be nice; it won't really matter anymore where I go in ashes form. That's not going to happen though; I don't plan on dying or feeling pain. The hair will be annoying with bald patches, but apparently that's 'endearing.' Thank you to all those who offered me words of love, support and kindness through this tough time. I would not be so strong without having intelligent people who I can have open conversations about this with and who can meet me without fear and hesitation in the dark places we all need to go to sometimes. All of them cheer me up at different times and in different ways.

27th February 2011

Four days before I go into hospital, eating out of anxiety: crisps, bread and chocolate... I need to relax so I watched Black Swan last night but could not take my mind off my operation. I thought that I was playing three roles at once; Beth - the one that ends up in hospital, the black swan; wild crazy girl out for a good time; and the good girl that's vulnerable and controlling then turns evil. Not much privacy at the moment but that's good, I don't necessarily want to be alone... but I wouldn't mind it either. Nothing anyone can say or do will help me feel better at this stage; I am constantly on automatic mode and those around me reflect this denial.

Part Two- Back to life

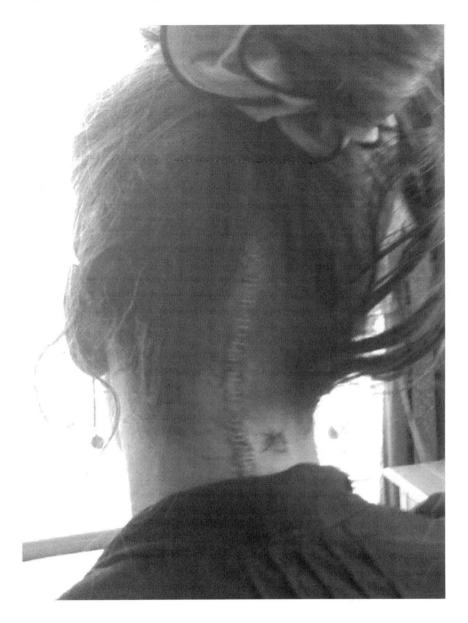

Chapter 7- It hasn't even been a week yet

Please note this section of the book is not for the faint hearted, and yet it needed to be included.

11ᵗʰ March 2011

I was discharged on Tuesday at lunchtime, exactly four days after my operation. I kept a diary while I was in hospital by typing on my I-Pad. I was on a cocktail of drugs including intravenous paracetamol, codeine, morphine and steroids. My euphoric moods which led me to posting on Facebook that I had just: *'Survived brain surgery'* are a side-effect of the steroids. It is so good to be home. I feel like I am finally starting to slowly relax. My neck still feels stiff and Wednesday was the worse day ever. Everyone is so impressed with how quickly I am recovering but I couldn't sleep properly last night and kept thinking: *'What's brain surgery like? Just think of the worse hangover you ever had in your life lasting over three days'* and: *'Why do caged birds sing? Because they are on too many meds!'* I know that doesn't make any sense right now, but I thought I would write it anyway. It hasn't even been a week yet, but I am already keen to get out and about. My family and friends, and

Jason, have been FANTASTIC I couldn't wish for more. I will post my hospital diaries soon.

It is worth mentioning here that although I got out of hospital extremely quickly I fainted the next day after I was discharged and I had fainted in hospital. I was extremely fragile at this stage and re-gathering aspects of my former self. I had wanted to die the day after I was discharged because of the extreme discomfort and because it constantly felt that my eyeballs would pop out of my head. No one had told me much about recovery and I am sure this is one of the parts of the story that I would rather forget.

I had a bag draining fluid from my brain for two days but I insisted on taking a shower the day after the surgery. As soon as I could walk I walked around carrying this bag and tying it up in the bathroom to have a shower. Even though the bag was taken out on Sunday, two days after the surgery, I was constantly paranoid I would accidentally pull it out in my sleep.

Nurses kept coming in and taking my blood and my blood pressure all the time while I was in hospital. I cannot imagine what my parents, my boyfriend and my brother must have gone through at this stage as they took turns spending long hours with me in hospital. I tried watching movies but I couldn't concentrate. I looked like a fragile zombie in a hospital bed playing angry birds on my I-Pad. (I don't like this game anymore.) I feel this experience has been as equally traumatizing for them as it was for me, and changed me in significant ways.

13th March 2011

I feel happier, stronger and the staples are out today. I can finally wash my hair; there is only so much dry shampoo a girl can use. Here are some hospital diaries taken from my I-pad:

I was terrified to begin with, the night before my angiogram and hospital admission I tried to get as much rest as possible, I spoke to a few friends and they were very reassuring. When I was with Jason earlier I just wanted to run away. My friend Andy said that sometimes when he would go to Iraq knowing that he was loved by people and that they wanted him to be well, it helped. It helped me but I also felt I wasn't choosing the experience and wanted to check out. From being an incredibly isolating experience to begin with I took great strength in every message of love and support just knowing people cared about me. It felt surreal. I checked into hospital at 7am on 3rd March 2011 and they were taking swabs, drawing blood... Then I had to dress up in the horrible hospital gown and massive paper underwear to go into theatre for my angiogram. The nurse came in to make sure I was shaved down there which I was warned of by my friend who is a nurse. They started poking tubes into my arm and asking me samba questions to keep me distracted. The doctor explained they would give me a local anaesthetic and put a tube from my groin all the way up to my brain. I would then feel a warm feeling once they switched on the contrast. They gave me a consent form to sign explaining the risks, which included stroke. I signed the form but before this they asked if I wanted a sedative or if I was going to tough it out. Of course I opted for the sedative. I remember the doctor who did it had to press down hard on my femoral vein, then seeing my boyfriend shell-shocked when I got wheeled out of the room wearing an oxygen mask. I probably looked even more shocked than him but I was very high on sedatives. I remember I felt like a goldfish, holding my breath while they switched on the contrast in my brain. I could then see all the veins around my head highlighting on the screen like a sci-fi movie. I believe this would help them map out the operation so that they would not cut any major veins. My parents had spoken to the doctor at this stage and he had given them some reassurances like they wouldn't put a catheter adjacent to my inner ear, and *'I wouldn't lose a night of sleep over this'.* These were some of the doctor's comforting words to my parents. I don't know whether this is ironic.

On Thursday, my leg was very sore and the surgery was to be scheduled at 11am the next day. I felt extremely anxious as I am sure everyone did. The doctor came in, the anaesthetist came in, I asked for a sedative but he said no: *'We want people fully awake very quickly after brain surgery.'* I hugged my parents and my brother, not knowing what to say or whether I would see them ever again.

Jason held my hand until I went down to the operating theatre; then they put me in a little room before going into theatre itself. Some guy untied the back of my hospital gown and put electrodes on me whilst the anaesthetist got me to inhale some oxygen and popped something into my vein, this was 11am. At 4.30pm I woke up shocked, retching and vomiting but with no pain, just throwing up. The doctor was wearing a suit and I remember feeling confused about this. He probably got changed in order to go and speak to my parents. Well I was alive! He showed me the picture of the cyst on his mobile phone and asked if I was on any contraceptives, to which I said no. Later on, I found out the significance of this question and why it is not a good idea to have a major operation when you are on your period. I had lost a lot of blood and become even more anaemic. I must have been in the operating theatre awake for over 40 minutes before going to the high dependency unit. I saw my parents' faces of relief and I had tubes coming out of everywhere. My lip was very swollen because they put a tube down my throat.

Given that I had lost a lot of blood, they had considered giving me a blood transfusion but luckily the doctor decided against it.

HDU overnight: Friday to Saturday

After I woke up and threw up, they wheeled me into HDU (high dependency unit). I had five tubes coming out of my body and I was most annoyed about the catheter inside my bladder. I saw my parents, Jason and my brother briefly and they looked so relieved to see me. During the night the nurses gave me intravenous paracetamol twice because I just wanted to fall asleep, but it was hard with the patients next to me. I could hear people next to me in a much worse state grunting and moaning all night. Later I found out that the woman next to me was being resuscitated and the guy who they moved me adjacent to had a big part of his brain missing. This really helped put my operation into perspective and realise how much worse it can get.

Unable to sleep, I would sit there and count the hours until the morning. Eventually, I asked for codeine and she told me it was an intra-muscular injection and it would be painful. I changed my mind but the nurse said she had to give it to me now because it was a prescribed drug. The other nurse told me that she had brain surgery in October last year, I did not want to hear about her experiences. Her experiences sounded very traumatic though and she seemed initially glad to look after me. I could not wait to get out of HDU. I was counting the hours and she would take her time in removing my tubes. She said if I ate without throwing up she would remove my drip. I ordered breakfast and slowly they took the big needles out of my veins because the doctor had agreed. Thank God he agreed not to give me a blood transfusion. I think the nurse was impressed with my progress as her surgery was more severe and she was in ICU for a week. I saw my parents and my boyfriend who said I looked better and waited for me in the other room. I felt so relieved the tubes were gone as that meant I was getting better. My friend Andy came to see me and it was great to have a giggle, he just walked into the HDU room, I am not sure how he got in there. I made a joke about my 'hat'. My lips were very swollen and because I could not sleep that night I asked one of the nurses for some Vaseline. He gave me a white tube and I spent all night staring at the clock and putting this Vaseline-like substance on my lips to reduce the swelling. I had not realised the cream was white and by the time the nurses came in, I had very big swollen white lips! *'What happened to you?'* the nurse said, while my doctor seemed unperturbed.

Overall, what a terrifying ordeal. The operation was on Friday from 11am to 4pm and I was back in my room with only a catheter draining fluid out of the back of my head on Saturday at 12pm! My parents were relieved. I lay in bed and asked for oral paracetamol then had a shower sitting down as someone still had to hold the bag. I had to lean on the nurse to walk to the bathroom. I could tell this was a difficult experience for everyone, my brother couldn't look at the bag and Jason found very hard letting go of my hand before I went into the operating theatre. I was worried about him. I was worried he didn't love me anymore because I looked so horrible. This is not actually the case and we are no longer together, but those were the thoughts that went through my mind while I was fighting for my life.

My mom went to get some clean clothes and gave me a lovely card from her and my father that really touched me, and I got some chocolates. Since it was Easter I would get a lot of chocolate and put on all the weight I lost after going *nil by mouth* for two days.

Sleeping was uncomfortable because I was scared of pulling the catheter off by accident in the middle of the night. I also had a nurse coming in to check my blood pressure and give me steroids every few hours. I was scared of having my catheter removed and getting stitches under local anaesthetic. This morning the doctor came in and decided to remove my catheter. First he said he would leave it one more day, and then he decided to remove it. He took my bandages out and gave me two local anaesthetics on my neck. I felt the fluid and I felt the stitches. Then they came in to take my blood again. I must add here that it was not a pleasant feeling at all, but in times like this I just had to surrender and make the best out of an uncomfortable situation by not fighting the agony.

When the doctor pulled the catheter out I felt a horrible pressure on the front of my head, especially behind my left eye. The doctor made small talk about living in Sydney and his daughter working near where I live. I just wanted to rest after he left but the physiotherapist came in and bossed me out of bed. She drew the curtains and tried to make me move my neck, got me walking around the corridor. The physiotherapist got me doing a lot of exercises, I remember one in which she would hold her finger up and down and get me to close my eyes and state whether the finger was up or down and I kept on getting it wrong. My brain was going through a lot of adjustments at this period; possibly expanding into the space left where they removed the tumour from. I felt ok after that. I still can't walk very fast but I had a shower standing up. My neck mobility is slowly getting better and the mucus in my throat is settling down. I think the balance will come with time. I am so glad this is over and I am making a speedy recovery: thank God! My friend Ruth came by after lunch and brought peppermints, it was really good to see her. She cheered me up and said she expected to see me semi-conscious on the bed. I know this has been a miracle and it changed me, but I am unsure of all the ways it has transformed me yet. I am very happy the recovery is going well and I feel positive and brave, I am taking steroids, looking forward to recovering at home and being 100% fit, healthy and strong again.

On Tuesday lunchtime I was discharged and allowed to go home. I saw two friends on Monday who cheered me up immensely, even though I fainted during the physio on Monday morning. The physiotherapist was pushing me to move my neck and I just saw her face go blurry and woke up on the floor. I had never fainted before in my life, and I vaguely remember her holding my body up while a lot of nurses rushed to help. On Tuesday it was Jason's birthday so he was happy I was going home. On Wednesday morning, apart from a very stiff neck, I felt fine, got up, thought about having coffee and then washed my face. I suddenly felt nausea and fainted. I fainted and smashed my head against the bath. I shouted and my brother and dad came to help me and put me to bed. Wednesday was the worst day, my neck was swollen and very sore, I had headaches and I could not lift my head off the sofa. I am so glad Wednesday is over. My parents took me to hospital Thursday and the doctor checked the bandage and said fainting is normal and that's all normal: *'You have just had major surgery, most people would still be in hospital'* he said.

Chapter 8- Making sense

22nd March 2011

If there is such thing as a 'survivors club', where is my membership? This was definitely a Grade A trauma and I am not doing it again. My friends are impressed with my recovery and no one can tell what I have been through just by looking at me. I am very keen to go back to all my activities and I get a bit frustrated with my lack of energy or the fact that my scar is still a little swollen on the top. It is a huge scar, but my hair will cover most of it. I went to a restaurant nearby to have lunch with my parents. I walked very slowly and could not move my neck sideways. I ordered some spaghetti and realised that this was a mistake as I could not look down at the plate because my neck was extremely swollen. Eating spaghetti without moving your neck is quite an experience. The same for brushing my teeth; I need to spit into the mirror and use my knees to bend. Changing clothes is also challenging when you can't look down. The tiredness comes regularly and I am sleeping all the time; I wake up to have breakfast, sleep, have lunch, try and watch a movie, sleep, have dinner then sleep again. The feeling of nausea is also a constant, whenever I eat I feel slightly ill afterwards. I forgot to mention that I had sea-legs in the hospital after the operation; it felt like my bed was a boat lost at the sea and it would not stand still. I gather that the cerebellum is responsible for all of these feelings of ghost movement. Following my operation it felt like someone had put me inside a blender on full power and then got me out and told me to walk straight afterwards. I felt I could barely zig-zag my way towards one direction.

On Sunday night I sneezed and all of a sudden I started hearing a very loud pulsating water noise in my right ear. The same thing that was there before my operation, but even louder. I called the doctor on Monday and I said to him that I can hear a very loud pulsating noise in my right ear. My parents were worried and told me to call him. I asked the doctor: *'What could it be, is it a blood vessel, or?'* *'That's the sound of you worrying too much Fernanda.'* was his reply. At least he had a sense of humour about my situation.

Let me mention briefly about the staples. The staples were removed a week after my surgery. With all 32 staples, I looked like a cyber punk with a metal Mohawk. I looked like I could be a raver at the Cyberdog shop in Camden-Town, London. Whoever stapled my head back together really went 'staple happy'. The staples were all stuck closely together. As I went into the hospital to remove the staples, I was wearing black to match the occasion. Just when I thought the pain was over, it wasn't. The nurse was very kind but every time she cut off a staple and pulled it out it was very uncomfortable to say the least. I don't drink tequila but I found that thinking about tequila shots helped me soothe the pain. Everyone was shocked when she removed the bandages to reveal so many staples. Because it was at the back of my head I asked: *'How many staples are there?* I felt that if I had a number I would be able to hold my breath and brave the pain. *'A lot'* was Jason's reply. *'How many?'* I insisted. *'There is quite a few'* he said. Maybe he had learned the doctor's skill of not answering questions. Once she started removing them, the staples seemed endless, especially as she took them out of my neck. Instead of crying I just tried to put on a brave face and 'protect' all those around me by saying *'let's go to lunch at Preto'*, a Brazilian restaurant in Putney.

I still could not move my neck sideways and I met someone I knew at the restaurant, he gave me a big hug not knowing about my operation. No one could see anything because the wound was at the back of my head.

30th March 2011

Three weeks and five days since surgery.

I am very lucky... I need to remember this everyday and send my love and prayers for those battling more aggressive forms of brain tumours. Anything to do with tumours at the moment makes me feel sick to my stomach. I subscribed to all the brain tumour research magazines but I can't bear to look at them. I just want to go back to normal life right now; running in the park and studying.

It is still all too soon. I stayed awake until 2am last night because my scar was so itchy I couldn't sleep. Itchy is good, itching means it's healing I guess. The scar is no longer swollen. The doctor said that some CFS fluid had escaped but apparently it's scabbing now that the staples are out. I was freaking myself out before and reading things on the internet about risks of reoccurrence. Honestly, I would rather die than have another op like this ever again. Yet, I am sure that you do whatever is necessary given the circumstances because you want to survive. I was very naive. For instance: '*What are all these tubes doing in me; four in my arms, one between my legs and one in my head*', also the angiogram was horrible. Anyway I will live my life and never think of that ever again. It is very rare and the doctor said I am no longer in any risk and I should not be reading stuff like that on the internet. Use the power of positive thinking.

He said six to eight weeks after the op until I am 100% again... Here is where my non-existent patience should be used. I am tired in the afternoons and bored of feeling so tired... wake up, breakfast nap, lunch, nap... I don't like feeling so exhausted so quickly but its part of recovery. And the noise in my right ear... it's like having a bee inside your head, but apparently it should settle soon.

So this is a blog about optimism and hope. Whatever the meaning and true value of the story is will become apparent with time. I am healthy, fitter, stronger and happier and will go back to exercise and have full energy to study and work in no time.

Goodbye to 'cerebellar haemangioblastoma' once and for all,

soon enough I can do my hair as the scar disappears and life goes on....

6th April 2011

Four weeks and five days since craniotomy

It's the little things that shouldn't matter anymore that, because apparently I am not going to die from a brain tumour, all of a sudden matter again. Like having loads of energy to no energy in seconds; having to take a nap in the afternoons (which is common six to eight weeks post-op); having no energy to call friends; feeling frustrated because I can't get a blow dry; feeling frustrated because I am not moving away from a career at the NHS yet; feeling apathy towards reading about IPA (a qualitative research methodology) when I made all these plans the day before. The worse is seeing cellulite on the front of my legs which shouldn't be there but I haven't been to the gym in a month so my legs don't look too strong. Feeling I need to exercise but having no energy even though I know this is temporary.

Not being able to justify eating all the pasta and chocolate biscuits anymore because I am 'convalescing.' I was walking past a model on my street and felt really under dressed in comparison, given my loss of confidence. I want to partake in the business and competition of life; and all of that is a change since yesterday. I was feeling very Zen, thinking: *'Having this op really made me focus on what's important in life.'* Oh the sarcasm...

4th May 2011

Two months

It's weird to think that if I didn't have this surgery I would have died within six to twelve months. I guess something like this should change you, but I am not sure how it changed me just yet... I am definitely more determined, individualistic, stubborn and grateful: but also restless and unsettled. I feel that I am looking for stability and whilst there is a part of me that wants to get on with things and finish my doctorate, there is another part that just wants to go travelling and is not settled down yet. I am more respectful of what my body can do and its limits. Some symptoms still occur after I drink alcohol; like feeling upside down in the middle of the night and the water noise in my right ear... I guess I am still in awe of what happened, and still trying to get back to myself completely. I want to run and have tons of energy... It feels like someone has picked me up in the middle of the night by my feet and is holding me upside down. However, I am still young and have the 'world at my feet', so I am happy for that. Why do things happen? Their meaning will hopefully get clearer with time

Part Three

Chapter 9- Moving on from the experience

5th July 2011

I haven't posted for a while. What an experience. I feel quite alone and not sure what to do with it or about it at the moment. It was indeed a miracle and for that I am very grateful. It's been four months and one day. There are still some lumps and bumps at the back of my head; I still can't throw my head back without fearing some sort of dizziness.

I am moving houses next week; new changes, new beginnings. Maybe people think that I am well and that is why I am never asked about it. I am terrified; petrified that it will come back, although it is extremely unlikely. I feel up and down, angry and sad. Still sometimes I have nightmares that I am about to have an operation when I am stressed. The fact that they cut my head open, drilled a hole into my skull and stapled it back together is not something that I can easily describe. Yes it was a trauma, yes I never want to repeat it and at the moment, I am just carrying on with life. I was so determined to get out of hospital and move away from the experience as fast as possible that now I am unsure what to do with it. I get angry with friends who are having plastic operations for fun because I had no choice in having mine. I could have died... Next year maybe I will run a marathon to raise money for brain tumour research. (I changed my mind about this as I don't feel I need to prove anything anymore.) Below are some notes I wrote whilst reminiscing.

3rd August 2011

My eyes find it hard to focus. There is nausea at the pit of my stomach, and everything spins but stands still. I feel disoriented.

I know I said dying is easy... that you just don't wake up. That was a while ago. I really don't want to die. I know what it is like now when your body is doing something you haven't programmed it to do. I know what is like now, when a simple movement of the head makes you think you are going to faint.

I try not to be reminded every day of when I was told I was going to die. *'A sudden death'* were the exact words, if I didn't have brain surgery within six months to a year. What now seems like the distant past was only five months ago, almost.

That feeling is back today, after a trip to the hairdresser, when throwing my head back makes me feels like I will either faint or throw up. I try not to show it and see my face in the mirror blurry but flustered.

I had brain surgery I say... brain surgery is no big deal.

But it is. Read my diary and how I used denial to try and survive an ordeal which quite frankly I didn't know I was going to survive. And how now I am concerned on a daily basis to finish my doctorate or whether I am thin when things like that simply did not matter six months ago.

On Wednesday 9th March 2011 I wished I had never had that bloody surgery. I did not feel 'myself'. I had fainted and then I could not lift my head without using my hands. I wanted the world to fade and for me to disappear. There was no comfort in sleeping. I had paracetamol every couple of hours and a pressure behind my eyes. My death wish didn't last very long. Suddenly the return of simple head movements was a blessing.

'She just had major surgery, most people would still be in the hospital' were the doctor's words in answer to my parents' concern after my faint.

I will never forget the woman next to me in HDU being resuscitated. I will never forget the pleas of Joe's parents next to me who had half the top part of his head missing. I won't forget what fainting feels like, or coming back after a four and a half hour operation. Well, seeing my parents' faces of relief, my brother's shocked face and my boyfriend's face of relief and apprehension. The pain was not too bad, the scar will heal. 32 staples at the back of my head, six tubes stuck to my body and the bag draining fluid from my brain. All that will go. Luckily I am still the same. Some people who have brain surgery we know are never the same.

How would you react if you were 29 years old and you were told you have a brain tumour and will die unless you have a serious operation?

I had no idea either. I debated both options and contemplated denial for a while. I thought: *'we are all going to die, at least I will know what is going to kill me. Maybe I am meant to die, perhaps they swapped the results; I am sure the doctor got it wrong etc...'*

I had no expectations of what I would be like after surgery and there were no plans in my diary after the 4th March 2011.

But today, again, I am confronted with that feeling which makes me worry. Is death ever so near? Will the danger not just disappear?

No... I know what it is like to lead a small death and to pray every day for healing. I know what it is like to have a hole drilled in the back of your skull, lose conscience and fight for survival. *'I will eat breakfast, I will do anything to get out of HDU'* is what I felt in my post-op anesthetised state.

Going into surgery was the most terrifying moment of my life. There is no rhyme or reason at that point. You can only hug those you love who are too shocked to cry or say goodbye.

Am I lucky, or unlucky? I just want to put it behind me.

But where is the sense in it? When it just doesn't make any sense that one day you will be confronted with the fact that you have a brain tumour: that you need to make choices fast.

It is only when I read about reoccurrence when I worry myself sick, and when I hope and pray every day that I am near a clean bill of health. I avoid doctors; I don't think about it, I don't talk about it.

I preoccupy myself with age, am I making the right choices, am I wasting my time, when will I have a break?

Sometimes I try to find a spiritual resolution, be thankful for what I have and wait... wait these feeling will pass. I don't ever want to mistrust my body again, struggle and stumble out of situations before I faint or die.

But I don't want to die... and in my experience, dying is simple. I am no expert on the matter and God I wish I won't be for a while. I have taken my health for granted, I have pushed my luck. Yet nothing could have caused what I had, nothing could have prevented it. It is rare, and thankfully benign.

The woman's face during one of my first scans, and the people behind the control in the MRI room, they treated me like I was about to die. *'You know how well or not you are'* they said. Of course, I didn't.

It is only a thin veil between life and death. The rushing around and aiming for goals. The working hard to accomplish my dreams. And death, a simple faint, a shutting down of the right ventricle; I don't know. The hospital madness I wish to avoid. Don't we all? Nobody of a sane mind wishes to die young.

I was out of hospital three days after the operation... At the same time, am I as strong as I think I am?

I was tested, and re-tested. I had enough testing. Please let me just get back to normal.

Soon after, I thought: *'No matter what happens, I will never have an operation like that ever again'*. That I would rather die. But that is a lie: of course I would. Every stitch and every needle, every gamble and every hope, every catheter and every staple. Every single drop of blood, every cut, drill to the bone, stretching of skin, every ache and every faint. If it means I can see those that I love again, and see them smile. If it means I can live: because dying is simple. Fighting is the hard part.

I know most people don't get a chance to reflect on their near death experiences, let alone have one. I know millions suffer with brain tumours too and I am not alone. Nothing prepares you for those moments and no words ever will. When everything just fades away... and you try to hang on because you know that loving life is all that matters.

Seeking meaning, consolation and hope, when you know that being angry at life is futile.

I remember counting down the days to brain surgery... Unaware of the risk, we were all in denial. I know now that miracles are possible and we must be grateful for our daily existence. It can easily and quickly flip over.

And I still need to remind myself of that sometimes.

15th August 2011

An angiogram: having a tube inserted from your groin into your brain... they switch on the contrast. Take the sedative I tell you... at least it will feel surreal... not real and so invasive. Morphine, then codeine stabbed into the muscle in your arm. Endless hours applying some Vaseline to my lips, staring at the clock... Pupil's dilated, lips swollen from intubation. And what was it like coming back?

Does that make me special? I just want to be ordinary. Yes they split my head in half with a knife, drilled a piece of my skull out and stapled it all back together again. Someone has been in my brain... and yet, I am still here; still the same. Still alive... still did not become enlightened by the experience. But I am changing every day. I can talk about death without hiding or shying away from the experience. My clients will talk about their pain, and their trauma... feeling special and entitled to their suffering... but really me too. Sometimes people are severely affected by much less. I hold on to both sides... life can always get worse; it gets better all the time.

A client said to me: '*We live in an unfair world, where children die!*' I know... Then you and I are dying a little every time... How you choose to live with that knowledge is what makes you live a successful or arbitrary existence.

Brain surgery is a blessing in a way. I can now live a more fulfilling life. I am not obsessed by death but I've been pretty close to being able to hold it in the therapy room, without trying to change that simple fact.

Chapter 10- What is left of me?

25th January 2012

This is the last section of the brain surgery diaries in excerpts taken from the time of the surgery.

I haven't posted here since August 2011. This is me, no holds barred, speaking from the heart.

Where do I start? I have just listened to Gabrielle Bernstein's Hay House streaming show on Miracles and Manifestations. She played a role in the early stages of my spiritual awakening. The ending almost made me cry. I loved her book Spirit Junkie and I hope to see her in London. Also, Andrea Foulkes, for those who don't know, is a wonderful past life regression therapist based in London. I will refer to the work I did with Andrea at a later stage in this book.

I am 31 years old tomorrow and in December 2010 I was diagnosed with a brain tumour. I was anxious, scared and all over the place. The doctor told me that if I didn't have this surgery I was going to die in six months to a year's time. I was in denial until I went to Brazil and spoke with another doctor who wanted to operate on me right there and then. I felt he wanted to pretty much butcher me for money rather than to operate to save my life.

I went to see John of God who is this worldwide famous Brazilian healer based in Abadiana, Brazil in January 2011. I hadn't been to a spiritual person beforehand, I used to drink and lose myself in the illusion like most of us. John of God told me to come back in the afternoon. He holds two sessions, one in the morning and another in the afternoon. He basically asked what I was there for, and I told him I had a cyst in my brain. He replied that: *'It was all removed'*. He says he doesn't heal, that God heals but I felt uplifted and inspired.

I must say that I was never scared. I thought death would be ok. I also had a dream about John of God before going to see him. In my dream he told me I would live to see old age. From a space in which I thought: *'It's OK to die'*, I was in Brazil thinking *'BUT I HAVE SO MUCH TO LIVE FOR!'* so I had my operation in March 2011 and I survived. I woke up full of catheters and tubes but I never cried. I cried on 8th March 2011 when I went home and my brother's friend came to visit. I didn't want to see anyone because I thought I looked terrible and I felt so battered and fragile. I went into my room, slammed the door, sat on the bed and cried. I survived this terrible ordeal which was also the best thing that has ever happened to me. It was a wakeup call. It was a call to say: *'Listen girl, I know you are a psychologist and everything and you think you can heal people and rationalise their troubles away but GET OUT OF YOUR HEAD! Get out of your head and into your HEART and start living!!'* I am no victim, I am no hero but I did live a miracle. I am here because I chose to be, because I know that my mission was not complete yet.

Since then I have been trying to get a job. I was very annoyed about not getting a job and I was meditating and reading books when I sat down at my computer to look for jobs again. There had been a few rejections and I started looking at the Pleiadian Messages on YouTube. Something inside me said: *'This is your job!'* I know that I still have a lot of work to do with my own stuff and my own ego, but since I started meditating I have been guided to start a meditation group. Now when I meditate I can feel my solar plexus vibrating. I am getting out of my head and into my heart. I am no more or less special than anyone else reading this.

There are days I feel guilty that I broke up with my boyfriend after I recovered from my surgery, but even though he is a lovely guy and he held my hand when I was being wheeled into surgery I can't be with him out of guilt. I can't be with him if he doesn't feel right for me. I wish him all the best and love him from afar. I had to focus on me. The collective conscious and the Universe has brought me here today as it has brought me into contact with Andrea and Gabrielle, and it will bring me into contact with many others.

So if you are out there, thank you for reading this.

Universe= Collective Conscious

Thank you for taking this journey with me so far. I am 31 years old tomorrow and I am not dead, instead I am here. I am happy and I am connecting with my inner guidance system and my body like never before. Disconnection brought me 'dis-ease' and I chose Light, I chose not to die. Today I am reading Gabrielle Bernstein, Chris Griscom, Kris Carr, Louise Hay and what they say makes so much sense. I was also led to many other like-minded people on this journey of transformation.

Part Four- Awakening

I would not call this e-book an autobiography as I do not feel this single experience defines who I am. At the same time, it has shifted my perception of myself and the world and made me focus on what is really important. This is what I seek to share in these pages. Having brain surgery has really facilitated my road to remembering my true nature and who I am transforming into. You don't need to go through something so drastic in order to be reborn. All you need to do is to shift perception. It is an allowing. It is a surrendering and letting go to become part of the whole. You were never really separate. It just appears to be so.

On the day before getting the results of my yearly follow up, I had a little panic about conflict and fear of further pain. As I stood near the library thinking about conflict, in my ego I really feared the pain. *'I just don't want any more physical and emotional pain!'* I remember thinking. Then the thought: *'Conflict, what is conflict?'* Popped into my head... Growth only occurs through conflict. You need to surrender and think: *'Bring it on!'* At this stage there would be a lot of dialogues between my ego and my higher-self. If I had tried to fight my way through brain surgery I would have ended up with a lot more battle scars both physical and emotional. Do not be afraid of the pain. Just stand in the sunlight and try and get as much light inside you as you possibly can.

If this is an illusion we need to de-programme and remember how powerful we are. This is an awakening. A lot of people are awakening at this time and the entry gate seems to be painful emotions, dissatisfaction and fear.

In my transitional state, once again before getting my results I noticed unhappiness in my body. I was at work thinking of how I wanted to be home; if I was home I would be eating sushi, having a bath and then getting into bed. The erroneous belief I had, which was producing my unhappy state was that if I had those things I would be ok, I would be happy. Later on when I got home I noticed that whatever I had was in order to get something else. I was just not ok, I was not happy in the present moment.

I toyed with this idea of needing to be somewhere else to be happy. I closed my eyes and dis-identified with the mind for a minute. I thought all those things 'sushi, bath, home' were add-ons. It doesn't matter whether I am here or there, it is the same; it is consciousness perceiving itself. I am all there is, and then there is the mind chatter, but it is so simple. The trees started to appear like holographic images and I had a big smile on my face while I walked home. I could be here, or I could be over there and it would be the same. When I closed my eyes I felt quietness and peace. This is all there is when you close your eyes. It is only Being.

Then, I revisited fear.

'Your scan is fine' says the doctor. 'Thank God!" I reply. Whenever I set foot into the hospital I get very nervous. I can feel my heartbeat quickening and my temperature dropping. I wondered how many people had actually died in there as I could feel a strange energy around my body. I am looking around the rooms, to the patients in their hospital beds and I can remember what it was like being there. I am looking to see if there are any nurses I recognize. I see a sign: *'Nil by mouth'* on a patient's door and I remember what it is like to be going through that experience also. I lost so much weight during the brain surgery. It is a very shallow thing to focus on but I remember being happy about that. I could eat what I wanted afterwards and yet the weight dropped off effortlessly. I was in a constant state of anxiety and fear. As soon as I recovered, I put the weight back on. My mother's friends would come over with cakes and chocolates and even though I felt constantly nauseous I felt I would eat in order to show that I was 'recovering.'

'But there is still some residual cyst left after the operation' continued the doctor. Again, because of pain your body takes over when you are being given bad news. It did not occur to me to ask him what that meant. Right after the operation, while I was throwing up because of the general anaesthetic, I remember the doctor showing me photos of the tumour he removed on his I-phone. I was very confused and could not make sense of it. I could not make sense of any of it. I looked at the clock and tried to tell the time. I looked at his phone and saw a rounded bloody mess. He showed me this image before

and after my follow up. The biopsy had revealed it was a begin brain tumour. He scrolled around his phone saying: *'Wait I have a better picture.'* I wondered how many pictures he took of this thing that was inside in my head. I wondered whether I could get him to send me a picture. Then it felt better not to ask. This is all in the past.

I sat there alone waiting for an explanation. I asked: *'Is it something to worry about?'* He said: *'no'.* The brain is an interesting organ, one that I cannot relate to very well as I cannot understand the images on the screen. Since the first time I saw an MRI scan it just puzzles me. It is not what it looked like in my biology books. Why does my brain look like a Dali painting? Why can't I get it to look 'normal'? I fired some more questions at the doctor such as: *'When can I do yoga or scuba-dive?'* He asked: *'You haven't got a shunt have you?'* I am not sure whether that was his sense of humour.

I left without asking the questions I really wanted to ask; whatever they may be. It is important to have someone with you during hospital appointments whenever you get bad news, because you will probably hear a third of it if not less. When he first told me a year ago that I would die unless I had the operation I remember just sitting across from him, apparently present. All I thought at that stage was how my hair looked good. The mind will block and deny and do whatever it can to protect you from bad news. This is why after hearing the news of a bereavement, people will often go into shock.

'No it hasn't changed in a year but you should probably have another scan in a year's time.' He stated. So I need to thank God every year after a scan when I am still alive. I cannot see the cyst on the screen. I thought he had removed it. I cannot relate to it as I can't see it. In my mind, in one version of the story I had while leaving the hospital, I am alone and scared. Another version tells me that this is a wonderful opportunity for further growth. Again I am battling between my ego and my higher-self. I chose the latter. Andrea's voice echoes in my head: *'We are here to master all facets of fear and sadness.'*

On the bus I am acutely aware of waves of emotions passing through my body. I am trying not to identify with any of them but they feel very real. First is fear which I can actually feel in my body as a flat emotion, making me feel heavy. Then anger and rage at the world in which I become a 'victim'. Then sadness comes like a huge wave. This is me in a transitional period where I am really grasping in the middle. Like a bridge between what I know and what I need to learn. Between ego, or my previous egoic identity with a story, and what I am yet to become.

It is Easter, the trees are still bare, the sun is shining and every Easter, like the Earth I shall be reborn again. My energy will transform. I take a deep breath: in with the new and out with the old, and I do this a few times. I am happy in my role as a story teller and motivational speaker but I do not wish to be retraumatised by my story. I need to find a way to let go. This is my way of letting go. I need to integrate all these versions of myself so I won't self sabotage. I know I need something bigger than myself to keep me connected and out of the shadow, out of the fear. I need to surrender and repeat this process over and over while telling myself: *'I chose happiness. I chose love, I love you, I forgive you and I chose to live!'* While I try to make sense of all of this, I know I cannot make sense of it in my head alone.

The world changes shape every time I hear the doctor's words: *'Cyst in my brain'*. What does that even mean? There are a lot of things in my brain: glands, neurons, fluid and yet the world becomes surreal. This could mean the world becomes more real. Between life and death I can make of life what I want it to be. We are all between life and death and this poses tremendous freedom. After the sobbing and the crying I am much quicker to rebuild myself. At this time I am much stronger and there is no denial. Something greater and bigger than myself uplifts and guides me. I can then let go of the story that no longer serves me.

Your thoughts and feelings manifest your reality. Do I know what is going to happen? Do I know what the future may hold? No. All I can do is to live by example and to hold the highest frequency and positive attitude in the now.

Fear is contagious and this is why I chose to let go of this story so that I do not worry about the future. A lot of my old identity, old relationships and friendships that no longer serve me have been left behind. I am no longer a vibrational match to victim mentality and fear. I only need to show up for myself. This shift in perception and conscious effort to stay in the present is a life saver. If I was to live in the future I would live in fear of a possible re-growth. All we have is now. I have learned the hard way that we choose our thoughts consciously or unconsciously and they can either manifest *dis-ease or* vibrant health. The choice is always yours to make.

I chose to embrace this rebirth and not relieve the experience. Once you get the message of what your body is trying to tell you, you can let it go.

Chapter 11 – Becoming

The Abraham-Hicks teaching in manifestation says that you need to practice a positive feeling until it is the thought that comes most easy. It is training yourself into expecting positive expectation. Yet, sometimes life throws you a curveball and even the most positive person can't maintain a happy attitude all the time. You can maintain an attitude of distant detachment, which is content enough. The challenge is the invitation to engage emotionally with the drama of life, which is a constant. The best thing to do in my experience is to feel the negative feeling fully, then remember what bliss feels like and align with that.

A professional rugby player I knew once told me about when he broke his foot so it changed position by 180 degrees. His instant thought upon learning that his damaged foot might have to be amputated was: *'How can I join the Paralympics?'* My response at the time was an emotional one, along the lines of: *'I don't know how I would cope with a broken foot.'* He then said that he would struggle if he had an accident which paralyzed him from the neck down, and stated: *'Then I would want to top myself.'* Here my response was the complete opposite, thinking of possibility: *'Well you could time travel, could you imagine... No responsibilities.'* His foot is fine and he continues to play.

Everyone is different in their perceived degree of resilience and everyone currently struggles to fully love and accept themselves to different degrees. However, young children don't come into this world with self-doubt. Young children love and accept every part of themselves fully. Somehow along the way, we tell ourselves we are not good enough, have a *'fear of failure'* and self-doubt sets in. Self-doubt and fear of failure are just constructs that illustrate fear, they mean nothing per se. Fear is an illusion: Fantasized Experience Appearing Real.

I believe it is possible to break out of the system. Break out of a job you don't like, follow your passion and get rewarded for it.

Healers must heal themselves first. Underneath anger you will always find pain.

I sent one of my friends a little video about entrepreneurship and his response was crucial: *'What does this guy know; I was out there being shot at.'* He referred to his experience in the Army and I started questioning why he was out there being shot at in the first place. In my experience anger, negative emotions and fear will get layered unless you nip it in the bud. By that I mean acknowledging and making peace with it. Most days, I am strong; but I am still making peace with my story. I am still letting go as I write this. Another friend, recently bereaved, told me that some things will never go away, that they just need to be accepted.

As I mentioned before, this is not a 'poor me' book because we all have our own crosses to bear. Right now, as I resume dating it is hard to be fun and exciting when I still feel a little bit wounded. I haven't got it together and I want to make this clear. I get lost and I get it wrong. Like learning a new language, this takes practice. The internal voice is always there inside me telling me how to reconnect. It is always present. The feeling that I am on the wrong path sometimes when I get diverted is very loud and helps me to get back on track. When I choose to ignore it, normally to avoid pain, things tend to get worse for a while. It just feels so much better to be in alignment. This is the skill of my new spiritual language which I am learning to tune in and out of. On the other hand, life is to be enjoyed and everyone will make mistakes from time to time. It is what we are here for and part of the learning.

I want to be on this Earth and I want to live. Every Easter is now an opportunity for me to move towards becoming all that I can be. I will be reminded to say thank you that I am alive. The day after my yearly check up, after I found out that there was still a bit of a 'residual cyst' left in my brain I was trying to reconnect with a power greater than myself. I heard a voice loud and clear in my mind telling me to go to church. I hardly ever go to church except for passing through, so I decided to honour this feeling and went. As I walked in there the priest was conducting a mass. People queued up and I heard again: *'Queue up'.* I queued up and got the Corpus Christi while the priest's pale blue eyes glanced at me. I felt much lighter after this clearing experience even when I didn't know what it all meant. Then later on that same night I had a first date with a guy I really liked. I got very drunk and told this guy my whole life story straight away. I was very matter of fact about it, but not only was I emotionally intense but I also tried to analyze him, and then kissed him. This is because sometimes I could easily cry about it, collapse about it and then it can feel that keeping it together and pretending I have it all under control is much harder. I admit that I don't have it under control at all and that I surrender to uncertainty. When I am in fear, happiness is a choice that I consciously need to make.

Following my date example, romance is the ego's playground. After this date I was to see this guy once more and because I didn't look my best my ego told me I didn't hear from him again because '*I wasn't good enough*' or '*I didn't look good enough*'. I believed this briefly then I let it go. I was also projecting the problem onto this guy before learning my lesson. Now, as the Course of Miracle says, I believe every relationship is an assignment and I question: '*What do I need to learn here.*' In this case it was to love myself a little deeper and not blame myself when relationships don't work out. People are not constants and most will change and come up with something new every day. I was channelling all my anger into exercising at this time. I also feel that this guy, Michael, was unhappy and depressed and he activated the 'rescuer' role in me at the time.

The experience I have gone through is opening up new ways of being with and of relating to people all the time. It is a much accelerated, evolving process. Being in touch with my own pain and mortality means I am now very sensitive to the pain of others. My doctorate thesis has been pretty much about me trying not to just give up and die, but I don't expect anyone to rescue me. I found that what happened is not something that defines me and yet it is something that I need to live with every day. Healing will take as long as it takes. While I am still healing, creating new intimate relationships is very hard. Nothing gels and I will push people away as much as I need them. This reminds me of wounded animals. When you have a wounded animal it is said that it will often attack those who try and rescue it. I think people can become attached to their pain, and the wounded animal will try and instinctively defend itself. Of course I wouldn't want to change my experience for anything. At the same time the split exists inside me and I would cry about it while my ego made assumptions as to what was fair and what wasn't.

Existential philosophy teaches us that life is paradoxical. Victims can often be perpetrators. You cannot have the good without the bad; God without Evil. And I know my strength comes from my weakness.

I am not separate from you reading this; I am merely a part of consciousness experiencing itself. Sometimes I feel separate and yet somewhere along the spectrum of awareness I am both big and small. I feel that I have earned my wings now but this would never be something for me to decide. The body is key, the body will tell you everything you still need to know. My brain hasn't done with me yet; there was still something I needed to learn here, and of course the learning or remembering can be endless until you finally get the message.

It is worth mentioning that although I sound over dramatic in some parts of this chapter, I am not being totally serious when I use my dramatic effect. Because I had not completely integrated my experience at this stage, I was attracting people who were a vibrational match to my own ambivalence, like a mirror.

Chapter 12- Happiness is your given right

I hear the full moon is especially big tonight. Although I haven't seen it myself, I tend to feel more creative when it is a full moon so here is another chapter.

I heard Marianne Williamson's London talk where she said that we will create our own Armageddon to help us evolve consciousness. My Armageddon had to be brain surgery. Of course, it had to be brain surgery to make me sit up, pay attention and start seeking answers. I have died and reincarnated many times during this lifetime.

I have been a lost child in Brazil who could see auras, to a lost teenager in Holland smoking weed, and a quasi-academic in London who had a period of being a semi-groupie. I had a recent phone call from someone who worked with a famous NLP life-coach practitioner trying to confirm my attendance at a workshop I had forgotten about, which went a bit like this:

C- I am calling to confirm your attendance at X's workshop tomorrow

F- But it says he is not gonna be there?

C- No, but this guy who is a published author and has worked with X for many years will and he will help you overcome your fears

F- But I haven't got any fears...

C- Everyone has fears

F- No, I know what fear is like and I haven't got any fears

C- But for humans there is always the next level and he will help you get to that next level

F- I know what the next level is and how to get there

C- So are you coming tomorrow?

F- No

At the time this was very funny for me. Of course, I knew what fear was like; being told you are going to die unless you have an operation in three months time is as close as I got. I could have searched and found some illusionary fear or I could have let him manipulate me into buying, but I chose not to.

Once Andrea also talked about the cosmic giggle, when you choose a 'trauma' to accelerate your evolutionary journey. Part of you is horrified, terrified and victimized. There is another part, at least in my case. A little voice, very small at first says: *'This is just f- great Fernanda; yes, well done!'* Almost laughing at the situation you got yourself into because you know exactly why. Of course for me, at this stage, the next level was astral travelling, but I was not going to tell the man that. Life had become something I could play with and be free within; like a treasure hunt. You cannot treasure hunt in a garbage bin expecting to strike gold.

I spent weeks catching up with my spiritual development on Facebook, YouTube, with books and meditation. I felt I had to write the results of my doctorate thesis by the end of the month. Instead, I would sit at my computer and watch YouTube clips, be lead to a myriad of spiritual teachers, listen to podcasts and read books. If they were telling the truth, they would all be saying the same thing. I learned about human history, the sacred geometrical shapes, spirit guides, astral travelling, the truth about the moon, the shift in consciousness. I didn't really learn anything new, but remembered. If something was 'true' it didn't matter how silly it seemed to my conscious mind, a little part of me would say: *'But of course.'* It was that little part of me that I was beginning to trust. It is this part of me that writes the higher aspects of this book following my rebirth.

It's midnight on a full moon night as I write this. I am learning so much about myself. The more about yourself you learn, the more of the Universe you take in, and again the more you learn about yourself.

I spent a day at my computer thinking I had to be somewhere else. The whole morning I felt I had to go and see John of God and thank him. I had to go and sit in his current and I will. The rest of the day I felt I needed to be in Australia. Then, I realised that I am exactly where I need to be at this point in time. You will meet the right people, at the right time and in the right order. I am exactly where I need to be at this point in time otherwise I would be somewhere else, like Thailand. If you are reading this, there is a part of you that wants to resonate or that is going through an awakening transition as well. Here is where I will tell you a little bit about how I ended up in London looking for my heart in a museum.

As mentioned, Andrea Foulkes is a past life regression therapist who I saw on TV back in 2008. At the time, I thought past life regression was interesting but I was very sceptical. However, as mentioned earlier, after having brain surgery I wanted answers and I wanted them fast. I wanted to know the reason behind all the suffering I had gone through. I wanted to pay my dues on a spiritual level. Now I know I have no dues to pay but that was really a blessing in disguise.

I met Andrea in October 2011 and we did a past life regression session where I found out I was a bearded man in a past life who worked on a ship and died of lung cancer. Of course, there is a part of you during a session like this that wants to believe you made up the whole story. I say: *'Don't throw out the baby with the bathwater'* because there will be a lot of links if you look for them. In another past life, I was a woman who drowned. Here there were a lot of messages internalised about not trusting people and it being unsafe to have an emotional connection. There were people I recognized in this lifetime and it helped me understand why, for example, I resented my brother when he was born (I love him dearly and more so as the years go by.) I was always afraid of water and I had problems breathing, and this was interesting because I had a vivid memory under hypnosis of drowning and drinking a lot of water. When I was regressed to the lifetime of the man on the ship, I had real difficulties breathing when I remembered the soul leaving the body and just hovering around looking at myself in my death bed. The feelings during the session were so strong that I felt that if I reached my chin I would feel my long beard. This is because Andrea thought therapists were difficult to regress being predominantly right-brained. I needed to remember and let go, and at that point I needed the stories.

At the time, I didn't get the answer I was looking for but I had other answers. I felt lighter, brighter and happier when I walked to the station after the session. It was like a heavy weight had been lifted from over my shoulders.

I saw Andrea again a few months after before I was due to fly to Australia. I decided to see her because I was feeling down again and while listening to one of her meditation CD's, my grandfather kept on popping up in my mind's eye. In a moment of desperation prior to surgery I had asked my grandfather to protect me; and he said he would be looking after me. During meditation, my ancestors and people I knew in this lifetime would appear when I would get to this temple during a guided meditation. They would show me things. This is why when a friend told me she goes to a psychic who talks to her grandmother I thought: *'Well you can do that yourself'*. I love my grandfather and it transpired that since I asked for his help he didn't leave. During this session I had to listen to my uncle's story, my grandfather's story and the guilt and sadness that ran in my family. I also had to let go of a few more entities that had attached themselves to me including a guy who had committed suicide by jumping off a building. For people reading this who are not familiar with past life regression work, this will seem odd.

It was clear that in my case there was a lot of 'heady stuff'. My uncle had been run over by a car when he was fourteen years old and he had undergone brain surgery to save his life. The doctors took a part of his brain out and he was never the same; he could not talk or walk for the rest of his life. This is a deeply sensitive and traumatic story in my family. This is why my surgery was traumatic for all of us on different levels, especially for my dad. My uncle was his younger brother. I need to add here that when trauma comes to the surface it is a good thing, it is to be acknowledged and healed.

Recently I switched off the lights in my room, doing an exercise I read about in Sheila Kelley's S-Factor. I put on Ryan Adam's song: *'When the stars go blue'* and just let my body move to the music, do whatever it wanted to do. I closed my eyes, there was no mirrors, no thinking just movement. The body is very wise, and as I moved my hips around a bit I started crying. I had healed on a conscious level and on a spiritual level, but my body was still catching up. My body remembered the trauma and it wanted to play it all over again. I let it do what it wanted to do which was mostly sit on the floor and cry. Similarly, I can now talk to my uncle in meditations and let it all go with love without holding on to any pain or trauma. It is all there to teach us the truth about Reality. I am full of gratitude for the role they played in my life; love is eternal and they are and have been mirrors for my own soul. During a recent meditation, I spoke to my uncle again and this time he appeared standing, young and fully healed.

I feel this is what Andrea meant when she said that when you think you have learned how to love yourself, there is a whole other level.

Let me mention briefly about connecting with nature, becoming invisible, my client shape shifting into the devil and looking for my heart in a London museum. At this stage of my transition I felt I wanted to get a merkabah tattooed on my back but I also felt that it may spin me out of this dimension. Please hang with me as it will all make sense as soon as you understand the transition of consciousness happening at a collective level.

It sounds like a horror movie how my client became the devil in front of me. Yet, the horror of when the vein behind my eye was pulsating or when I had a water noise inside my head was much worse.

This guy came to see me in private practice and although I cannot go into details about why he came to see me for therapy, suffice to say he didn't like himself very much. We spent a whole session with me trying to help him and he was either self-attacking, or attacking others. Then, I looked down at the floor for a second and a wave of fear crawled up my leg. It was almost as if I could see a tail and I knew that, if I looked up I would see him as the devil laughing at me. I composed myself and thought I had to ignore that. I searched inside me for what could be a vibrational match to this new manifestation. Why would I be counselling the devil? Nothing surprised me anymore. Because the veil between dimensions is getting thinner and thinner by the day should you open up to it? If you haven't started seeing things or feeling more then you probably will soon. (Unless you are still so defended and disconnected, then you will find the 3D illusion extremely challenging.)

I thought of quitting private practice for a moment. How could I have a psychological intervention with my client like:

F- So last week when you turned into the devil....

On the other hand, I was becoming invisible to things that were no longer a vibrational match to my changing frequency. I had been to Andrea's workshop in London and felt a bit spaced out because something else had awakened in my consciousness. At first I felt I had to be at a friend's birthday and when I finally relaxed I didn't want to be anywhere else. I could now see movements around people's heads, which had also happened before years ago. As my psychic abilities increased I struggled to stay in 3D because my body did not want to put up with alcohol or meaningless conversations. I don't like myself if I fall into old patterns, complaining about work or relationships. I had lost a crystal that same day, a rose quartz that wanted to belong to my personal trainer, and re-gained a crystal, also a rose quartz that I was carrying around.

When I went to the bar to look for my friend I could not find her. I searched and searched and the second I gave up searching my bus home appeared and that felt great. She was there, and I was there but because she was in a very different vibrational state our consciousnesses literally could not meet.

Then I realised that my reason for coming to London was a desire to punish those who had stolen my heart in a different lifetime. I had been talking about leaving London for a while, thinking my doctorate was the only thing that kept me here. Where would I go?

Andrea came over and I asked her for another one to one session. We were talking about moving around and letting go of responsibilities. She put me in a meditative state and I realised that in a different lifetime I had been a 14 year old boy who was defending himself in Egypt. I was captured, sacrificed and my heart was torn from my chest. I don't know whether this could have happened in those times or not, as I mentioned a little part wants to always remain a little sceptical at first. During this hypnotic state I felt so hollow. I felt hollow and I knew I had to be looking for my heart in a London museum. I was really keen on this mission and could see it in my mind's eye. I then reconnected with my heart on an energetic level assisted by Andrea. I can't really do justice to the complexity and theory of this spiritual work in words. Even when I write this now, I can hardly remember the feeling although the images stuck. For me, the heart was the missing piece. Now I was ready for the next phase of my transformational shift.

Chapter 13- Connecting the puzzle pieces

I spent the whole morning crying. Crying so hard that I became afraid the neighbours would hear me. I cried so hard it felt endless. It felt as if a vein in my head would pop. I cried so hard that I am still crying now. I cried so hard that I cannot sit in meditation because my nose is blocked. I cried so hard that I am worried how I am going to see clients later because my face looks so red and puffy. What am I crying about? Feeling rejected, feeling lonely, feeling like I am not good enough. I have to be completely transparent otherwise there is no point in this book.

The funny thing is, that whenever you think a journey has ended it has only begun. The crying was ok because I just had to release some more negativity before moving onto the next chapter. I felt so much happier after crying, it was like fresh spring after a thunderstorm.

So let's start at the beginning again. I remember that I have always been open to the 'spiritual side' of life but I learned early on to stifle that aspect of my personality in order to be 'accepted.' The paradox is that I wanted other people to love and accept me for all that I am but I could not love and accept myself at that point. At this stage 'brain surgery' feels like a distant memory and I cannot even connect to any pain associated with it. I have vague memories of the hospital but it is as if my memory has been erased. It is interesting how what I craved more than anything else was acceptance and yet I struggled to accept myself.

I studied psychology to avoid being bullied, to avoid being rejected, humiliated and picked on. It was a way of getting on side. It was the way that I would protect myself against others and not feel inferior because I would 'know' human nature. For twelve years that was my 'roadmap to happiness'. It was a roadmap to reality rather because it provided the answers that I sought in understanding human nature. If the existential approach would not explain why, then I would look at the psychodynamic approach and vice-versa. However, the existential approach looks at what and the psychodynamic approach looks at why.

I was feeling lost and confused and it didn't matter how many qualifications and letters of registration and accreditation I gathered after my name: it didn't feel 'good enough.' I thought that perhaps, in gaining my doctorate, I would feel good enough and I would breathe a sigh of relief. On the other hand, I was becoming increasingly frustrated with the doctorate and with academia in general.

Walking to the gym one morning I felt that my roadmap to happiness had changed. It was no longer about philosophy or psychology, it had become spiritual. However, not all aspects of 'spiritual' were included; I had to become discerning in what worked for me. For some people, their roadmap to happiness might still be philosophy, psychology or 'science'. It depends what stage they are at and what questions they want answered. I feel that the only wrong roadmap is a fear-based one. In that case, the person is lost. Although, it is ok to be lost too. We are not here to suffer but sometimes that is what it takes. We only grow from conflict. We chose contrast. It is like a conversation I had with a friend about dating 'bad boys'. Without the contrast we wouldn't know what a nice guy was and how we want to feel in a relationship. Opposites are there to give us perspective; we chose contrast because of that.

Therefore, my 'spiritual' roadmap was abandoned early on. Like most toddlers I spoke to spirits. My mother told me how while having a bath I would have conversations with spirits and then tell her about it. I had an imaginary friend in school called 'Ben' and in some ways I am sure he helped me feel less alone because I felt so different to the other kids. If we go back to the roadmap, it will be different for every single human being on this planet. What worked for me is not going to work for you and vice-versa. I used to think that some souls on this planet are very young and are here to play. Some souls just feel 'old' and feel 'different'. It is all exactly as it is meant to be. We are here to follow our bliss and to experience joy. I also feel that in order to experience joy we needed duality. In order to experience real joy and move away from duality consciousness we need to go into our hearts and feel unity consciousness. Only then will we create heaven on earth, and this is where we are headed. I am not promoting a particular school of thought or spiritual teacher, everyone's journey is meant to be different. I am merely describing what worked for me.

My dabble with my spiritual roadmap, which I labelled as unimportant at the beginning, would come and go throughout my life. I mostly repressed my spiritual truth. I played with

116

candles, I would evoke magic, I would bless myself as a witch and then I would try 'Satanism' before experiencing some very fearful phenomenon and getting on my knees to pray. I would only pray when I felt very lost and afraid or when I was in trouble. I would never describe myself as a religious person but spirituality was always in the background. As I transitioned and awakened I remembered having dreams of flying the whole Earth. I could go anywhere I wanted. With a simple jump and I would be on the other side of the globe. I flew over continents and rivers and it was the most liberating feeling ever. For some reason that memory stayed with me. I also remembered connecting with the stars in meditation. A few years ago when I lived in Holland I caught a glimpse of myself in the mirror and didn't recognize the image reflecting back at me. I lay in my bed and started asking myself who I was, starting with my name. I would gently repeat my name in my mind over and over when all of a sudden the Universe just expanded and I was out in the stars. It was the most amazing, expansive feeling ever. A few years later, I shut off. On the other hand, I know what expansion feels like, and it is a feeling I am willing to experience again, consciously as much as possible.

Therefore, whenever you feel the journey has ended, it has only begun. I am full of love and gratitude for all of the spiritual teachers I have come across at this stage of my life. They have all helped to awaken the memory inside me that I am a manifestation of the divine. I am an expression of the divine and so are you. These spiritual teachers are: Andrea Foulkes, Teal Scott, Eckart Tolle, Gabrielle Berstein, Louise Hay, Marianne Williamson, Abraham-Hicks, Bashar, Lilou Mace, Jordan D., Drunvalo Melchizedek, Leija Turunen, Lee Harris and many more. As Drunvalo Melchizedek would say: *'There are many ways of interpreting one reality'*. However, you have to break down the old pattern to get to the new pattern. Ascension is moving from the brain to the heart. This is where I was at. I wanted to fly before I could walk. I had to maintain an attitude of gratitude in my new expansion and stay connected to my heart. The past is not where you are headed, but whenever you feel the journey has ended, it has only begun.

Chapter 14- Waking up from the human drama

I realised that my job is to help people wake up from their human drama and realise who they truly are. All the letters after my name and my doctorate do not really matter. They only matter to the extent that it allows me to sit with people and help them to wake up to the fact that they are creating their experience and that we are all infinite consciousness and unlimited potential. It took me a while to get here. My soul must have thought it would be fun to spend twelve years studying psychology before I realised who I am and what truly matters. All the books I am reading seem a bit 3D in this new shift of consciousness and psychology no longer answers every question I have about humanity. I feel that all the hours I have spent and continue to spend reading spiritual books, meditating, and watching YouTube clips from spiritual teachers are research for my new job. The Earth is changing, and in order to accommodate this shift in transition we need to change with it.

The brain does not understand human history knowledge and the way we interpret reality in this manner is limited. I am excited about my new job and releasing old ways of being. I was reading an article my academic supervisor wrote talking about the leap of faith in the absence of God. I got a bit confused whilst reading this article as I could not understand the concept of: *'An absence of God'*. It felt to me at the time like a comparison would be a fish in the ocean asking: *'Where is the water!?'* I thought: *'How can there be an absence of God if you understand that Source and God are all around you much like the fish in the water'*. Interestingly, it depends how you conceptualise God and 'leap of faith'. You don't need 'God' in dogmatic religious terms in order to take a leap of faith. If you understand that in your purest essence you are God then you can have a leap of faith without God because it doesn't matter which way you go, you cannot get away from God. I was becoming interested in this new way of being and I knew that I still needed to release some more pain and old ways and get even more connected with Source in order to inspire people out of their fears.

I saw my ex-boyfriend over the weekend and it was a reminder of how far I had come. I felt he wanted to pull me back into fear and drama and I was smiling at him, having none of it. I told him the human drama can be very enticing and you can always find something to glue your fears and your tears to, but that's all illusory. I feel that I have been transformed. However, there is still some more work to do on myself. We are not done yet and it will never be perfect. I thought that I would reach a level where everything would be magical; I would have complete control over my emotions. I would know who I was, where I was going and I would be surrounded by abundance. I would finally feel like I belonged. I am not there yet. I am pretty much the kid in the playground who still doesn't know where she fits in and doesn't understand why the other kids won't play with her. I will give an example that illustrates this.

It goes from belonging, which in my life has always been a very quick and fleeting experience, to not belonging, which right now feels like my habitual way of being. Firstly, I must mention that since I started writing this book a few full moons ago I have only felt creative when there is a full moon. Today, on another full moon in June 2012 I sit down and the inspiration just seems to flow out of me. I don't fully understand the connection between my creativity and the full moon, but I felt I would mention it nevertheless.

Let's not play small here. Where you are is absolutely right for those around you. Refusing to shine your light and to speak your truth means you are depriving the world of your unique contribution. If you were already dead, what would you wish you had done differently? I appreciate that not many people are told they are going to die in six months to a year and then live to tell the tale. This does not make me special. I just had to get this book out there with all its imperfections. How come then do I still feel like I need to justify my existence on this planet like some invisible magical token of gratitude to ensure my survival? We are all unique and the same, but my ego wanted its moment to shine in some parts of the book.

Some great words from Mastin Kipp: *'If you can transcend your fear of death you can accomplish a lot.'* I have transcended my fear of death but I don't feel like I have accomplished a lot. I need to be creative. He said: *'You attract what you are.'* I was having a conversation with him in my head when an interview of his popped out of nowhere into my mailbox and I scribbled some notes down. Mastin said: *'Can you practice being love in this moment?'* Try it now!

For me it is hard, if I am surrounded by papers in rainy London, to think of how I am going to write the discussion section of my doctorate thesis; or rather not think about it. I am thinking instead of the biscuits in my cupboard and worrying about this and that. Worrying about tomorrow and worrying about how I am going to get this book proofread, how much that will cost. I am worrying whether the world is ready for my book, whether I can move and where to move to. I am avoiding thinking about things and feeling about things. I am worrying about how to divorce my parents, how to follow my dreams and I am feeling a bit down. The phone rings and it is one of my friends but because I am being a bit of a hermit and also because I am giving up alcohol I don't pick up the phone. I don't pick up and I feel a bit lonely as it's only me and my cat and I haven't got any romantic partners in sight at the moment. My heart feels empty as feeling attached to anyone right now is pushing them away. It feels like I can't love which is a ridiculous idea, even writing it down. The post-it note near my bed states: *'I want greater romance in my life.'* The paper near my fridge has a long list of qualities that I want in a partner. I feel I need to trust and I need to forgive. In a few minutes time I will go back to reading a book called: *The Angel Whisperer*. I will probably eat a cookie and wonder how I felt excluded from the Hay House group at London's mind body and spirit festival. Part of me knows that everyone at that festival was experiencing a very different reality. My reality was: *'I want to be where they are at, I want to be a published author, yet I feel excluded!'* My ego was saying: *'This is just a way of selling spirituality, a lot of people who claim to be spiritual and feel they are better than you and me have just fallen into a different trap.'* My ego is having a field day with this new experience; it says I am special because I almost died and because I have a doctorate. (My ego wanted its own moment in the spotlight in this book!) It feels dismissive of some people at the festival because I felt rejected by them, which is an inclination to say I want to be where they are at. My higher-self knows I am exactly where I should be and it tells me to just relax, that we are all playing our part.

Yet my ego shouts that they haven't got anything I haven't got and then changes that message, saying they do, and that I need to go into my heart. What is the secret? The secret is that at this point my writing is not clear which shows the schizo nature of the war against the ego. Let's love the ego instead. Let's say that I have accomplished a lot, and not dying is part of it. I will accomplish much more and I don't need to drag anyone down in order to get to the top. We can all accomplish together. It is a win-win situation if the best in me brings out the best in you and vice-versa.

Chapter 15- Not fitting in

I have always felt like I didn't quite belong and that I couldn't quite connect with other people in a way I believed others found easier. Some people can relate to this experience of feeling like an outsider. We are waking up.

Studying psychology for the past twelve years was not only an attempt to try and figure out what people were about, but also to protect myself from the pain of feeling excluded and rejected. I was never the popular girl at high-school, and it was only at university that drinking and my looks gave me a false sense of being 'special'. At university being Brazilian gave me an air of being 'exotic', and therefore people gravitated towards me. I used psychology as a weapon when I had any conflict with friends and lovers. Growing up, I looked like I didn't belong. There is a photograph that comes to mind where I must have been around seven or eight years old and I am dressed as an ant at a school play. I have a dark outfit and a dark cap with antennas. While most of the children look happy to be part of the play and embrace the role of the ant, I am looking around a bit lost and confused.

Similar memories come back when my parents put me in swimming classes and ballet. I was the one who looked around looking baffled and not part of the group. I had the outfit and I played the part to the best of my ability. When I fell in front of a large crowd and I saw all the adults pointing at me laughing, I must have been around twelve years old and, as opposed to crying and running away which is what I wanted to do, I pretended nothing had happened.

People at school also noticed that I looked different and used this as a means to ridicule me: I had short, frizzy blond hair. I remember going to school one day, feeling as self-conscious as any kid would in their teens, and noticing a group of kids on the top floor of the building pointing at me and laughing, shouting horrible things. I then decided I was ugly. I would play small and hide when I could. I wanted to be invisible so I couldn't get hurt.

Feeling like a freak because of my hair, or my features became a large part of my early years and I felt I needed to play small and hide. A lot of ugly ducklings turn into swans and I was no exception. At the same time, the kids being mean, pointing and laughing and saying horrible things do leave psychological scars that are not easy to forget unless you process them. How do we heal these relationships? We need to go into the pain and forgive. There is a part of me that still feels inadequate. I am learning to embrace this difference and the fact that I am not like everybody else. I am imperfect. The feeling that I was not pretty because I was not perfect used to affect me a lot. I hadn't noticed before how I seemed 'different' to other kids unless this was pointed out to me. I also made no effort to fit in and withdrew into my shell of being an introvert, keeping diaries, drawing and writing poetry.

Feelings of belonging only happened much later in high-school when I started smoking weed with friends. The weed made me feel a little less self-conscious about the fact that I wasn't perfect and that my English wasn't perfect. At that stage, I also noticed how everyone else was struggling with the same issue of acceptance so I cut myself some slack and, by the time I left high-school, I was feeling a lot more confident because I was dating attractive guys, proving to myself that I was attractive.

At the same time, some habits die hard and although I have a lot of love and empathy for myself as a child, I also notice how I can repeat certain patterns. Two recent cases occurred through my need to be liked and my need to belong. I would go into them but it suffices to say that we create our own experiences. Sometimes we manifest situations and people we feel uncomfortable about. This is a wonderful opportunity to go inside and realise what is really going on and why you are creating a situation that you feel unhappy about. I include this next section in this book so it can be seen how the ego perceives itself as separate and under threat.

I was very set on an American spiritual teacher and learnt a lot from her, but then she started to annoy me. This is only because she was mirroring aspects of my own personality I wasn't ready to own yet. There were too many videos, too many messages and too much self-adulation for my liking. I went along to see one of her talks anyway, but I was feeling rejected by one of her followers who I had exchanged a few emails with and had never replied after I sent him the link to my videos. My ego was therefore mortally wounded when I saw a photo of him, her and the 'Angel Whisperer' on Facebook. How was I to be Zen about this and get what I needed from the workshop, and at the same time not show how I was bitter and my pride was wounded? I went along anyway and she mentioned something about John of God. My opinion of her alternated from feelings of love and acceptance, to an annoyance at how much I felt she was self-promoting. (Which is my own issue, because if I didn't feel at the time that I had wanted to be where she was, I would not be bothered at all by this.)

I know now that I have mixed feelings towards someone on the spiritual path when I perceive them to be a mixture of light and darkness, and I can forgive her for struggling with her own ego as I am too. We are all only doing our best.

Anyway, as she spoke about John of God I lifted up my hand, claiming John of God to be one of my specialities too. My heart was beating very fast and I almost started crying. For some strange reason I felt the need to tell an audience of over 200 strangers how I chose to live and how I would assist in taking them to Brazil to meet John of God. Practically speaking, I don't see how this is going to work but somehow I felt guided to say what I did to the audience that day. I feel that the higher spiritual purpose of this will reveal itself at the right time, I just need to trust.

Being truthful about my own ego, I didn't know how to treat this woman who I had perceived as a spiritual teacher in the past. I gave her one of my favourite rose quartz crystals as a thank you token and left thinking: *'Why the hell did I give her my crystal? I loved that crystal and she just put it on the table like she didn't even value it.'* I felt battered and annoyed at myself, like I wanted to message her asking for the crystal back. On the same day, someone posted on her wall: *'Thank you for my rose quartz crystal you gave me from Brazil'* and I felt that was my crystal she gave away!

I was still learning to let go. I felt annoyed at how some people were put on a spiritual pedestal because they had what I thought I wanted, and that I wouldn't handle these situations in the way they did. As I watched two people who were in the audience embrace her to take a picture I was annoyed I couldn't go up to her and do the same. My ego felt I was better than that and also that I could have helped those two particular girls even better than she could, given my background in psychology. I am not proud of my ego projections. As I moved towards the light my ego was tripping me up right, left and centre.

All my old demons surfaced so that I could recognize and heal them. This was fundamentally a good thing as a few months ago I would not even have dreamt of meeting this woman. Now I wanted what she had and felt I didn't need to jump through hoops to get it. What works for one person is not necessarily going to work for others. We all have a different and unique contribution to make and we don't need to be anybody else but ourselves. I was clearly operating from an ego place here. As the Course of Miracles, and this lady would say: *'The Ego is suspicious at best and fearful at worse'*. This section is a great example of this.

My Ego;
Suspicious - that I'm not Sane
Fearful - that we'll never meet again

Chapter 16- From Glastonbury to the stars

I know that I might lose a lot of readers at this stage. If you are reading it's because you are curious about me on a level of conscious awareness, or because you are friends or family wondering how far I will go. At the same time, this is my truth and it needs to be told in full for this book to accomplish its intention. The intention is the one I chose as my purpose for this lifetime from the very beginning, or one of my intentions. We are multidimensional beings. We are spiritual beings having a human experience; some know this already, some don't.

If you don't know it yet... that's ok too as you will soon find out. You don't need to die to reincarnate. I had been dealing with my ego more than ever. Like peeling layers off an onion, the closer I got to the truth the more obstacles would appear and the more challenges and opportunities for growth would turn up. Would this be a never ending cycle?

For love, I would do it all again. For the love of humanity takes my heart. I would do every needle and every cut, every bit of blood and pain. If it's worth it, it's for love. I can joke about brain surgery now to acquaintances as I feel nothing. I don't feel the need to do it over again as I have learned what I needed from it. This book is for my future children and whatever art form will come of it. This book is for humanity, for we are all in it together. If a sacrifice is what it takes for people to wake up then I volunteer to sacrifice myself over and over and over again as I have done before; not as a victim or a martyr, in the service of knowledge. At the same time, that part is done. Now I can follow my bliss and align with others on a similar level of consciousness. My job is to shine the light and to be informed, sharing this information.

My job is to be happy and to stay vibrating at a high frequency. A section of this book as you probably know has been downloaded straight from the stars. The exact location doesn't matter, all that matters is my journey as a gift to the world. I am here to learn about unconditional love, to forgive and to evolve. Glastonbury is really calling me now; at first it was a whisper and now I wake up with it when I open Facebook and I meditate on the Tor before going to sleep. I know, I will respond to the call. I am enjoying being happy in the moment with my newly activated star seed friend. We met in the most unusual circumstances and there will be a lot more to this story. I am keeping this part of the story private for now as I heal my own feelings of rejection and abandonment.

Let's go back to John of God and when I received my healing. I was standing at the airport in Brazil, on my way back to London, when I noticed a sick man. From far away the thought of whether I could heal him by giving up my own healing in his favour popped into my head. I decided right there and then that I would in fact let him be healed instead of me and felt a wave of energy leave my body onto the floor. In that moment we locked eyes for a few seconds.

At the moment, all this spirituality stuff is a new language that I am still learning to decode. I am still integrating the old, letting go and clearing space for the new.

I appreciate that there are many ways of understanding all the tests I have gone through to get to where I am today. Part of being who I am here to be means that it is never a battle to choose someone else's benefit over my own. I know we are all infinite, we are all One, we are all Source and we are all connected; so why would I hold on to some illusion of healing myself at someone else's disadvantage? I choose love. I choose peace. I choose happiness for myself and for all of humanity. There is only a veil between us which is an erroneous perception. My healing of the world started first and foremost with healing myself.

Chapter 17- The death of the ego

It's funny how, when I think about ascension as a going home or dying, a part of me gets really scared. I know that I have died and we have all died a million times before. Once the human experience has given us all the knowledge we need, ascension is only the next step in evolution. The part that will fall away, that will die, is the ego and the ego is really scared.

It is difficult to explain a journey that is beyond this stage of evolution in simple 3D terms, but I will write what flows through me. The point is flowing, and once you have raised your vibration why would you want to go back. When I think about the ego dying, and I think about resistance to change, I think about my client work. I did a two-chair technique with a client recently, which comes from the Gestalt approach to counselling and psychotherapy. The idea was that she would speak to an empty chair addressing that part of her that is really resistant to change, the part that wants to self-punish and stay unwell. The other part, the part that wants to be the best she can be, was to address this more immature part of her personality and give it comfort, assuring it that change is ok and that it would all be alright. Immediately during this exercise she wanted to sit on the resistance chair and sulk. I asked her how old this part of her was and what it wanted to say. The part that resisted change was eight years old and she was scared that if she changed she would get told off, be rejected, ignored and have no friends. This part was also

136

terrified of uncertainty, preferring the familiar place where suffering was 'comforting.' I asked her to swap chairs and to tell her eight year old self that she loves her and that it will be ok if she changed to blossom into her full potential. She could not do this part of the exercise easily and still felt incomplete and attached to her suffering and her sadness. This is a good example of what I believe the ego is like with regards to ascension. You cannot ascend unless you heal your ego projections.

The ego is scared; it is terrified of what might come. In shining the light we must accept these darker aspects of ourselves. What is real cannot die, and what is real is not your name, your job, how much you earn, your story, your parents or the illusion that is all around you. It feels very real however, and we become attached to the play, to the characters and to the going back and forth looking for ways of 'completion.' I watch my ego as it wants to date again, to go back to bars and to go looking for something external that it believes will bring more happiness to itself. Nothing outside the self will bring more happiness to itself. The part that wants to evolve, unlike my client's resistance, really just wants to play in the sunshine, but this part is scared that it is going to take more work and that it is going to take more suffering in order to evolve.

Evolving is effortless when you align with your higher-self and allow the flow and the light in. I want to play with new friends at the same level of evolving consciousness. I want to feel the magic. I want to embody my soul. I want to know that I am not limited by my five senses. I want to give up all my jobs and responsibilities. I want to run naked in the woods. I want to swim in the ocean with the dolphins and I want to feel free. I want to enjoy physicality and all the joy it can bring. I want to feel whether this will open the gates to higher levels of consciousness. I am ready to give up difficulty and to say goodbye to those who keep me stuck. I want to be my divine feminine soul. I want to know that the flickering light up in the sky is what I think it is. I want to know that all my dreams are coming true because I am the unlimited potential of creation, because I am made of light, because I am a multidimensional being having a human experience. Part animal and part spirit. The spirit can cross all limitations and can travel through space and time. I want to meet others who are going to say yes, who are going to scream yes at the top of their lungs to this new way of being. It is the removal of all that is unreal and untrue that is necessary so that we can become our true essence; one not of a crystal but of a diamond. Yes!

It did take some suffering to get here, many lifetimes with different missions; but as we walk this Earth together hand in hand, it is to raise our vibration and the vibration of all the other souls around us. So forget about my story, forget about what I appear to be. Forget this beautiful illusion of parental love or the family I thought I had. I am ready to leave it all behind for what is new; what is real. In this language I am limited in my expression of words but I want to tell the ego that it is ok, that fear is simply an illusion that will fall away with the right focus and intention. I am ready to say goodbye to all that I know, to all that I am so that I can become part of the sky, part of the sea, a conscious part when the time is right. There is so much to experience on this beautiful planet Earth; there is so much to create. Beautiful surroundings, close to nature, free of all limitations where you can be connected to all that surrounds you. Where you can be one with the rain, one with the rainbows and the sunshine before returning home.

Remember, time is an illusion so you are as much home now as you were when you left. It took some brave souls to leave the boundless potential of creation, to go into human form and suffer repeatedly getting lost, before finding their way back to the light. Just be aware of perception. Perception is what is real. This constant observer in your head who's never left you who's always wondered why you chose the wrong perception over and over again, who showered you with unlimited love. The observer, who asked when you were 16 years old: *'Is this it?' 'Does that mean that when I die it will all be in vain? I will have no identity, I will have struggled in vain, my parents meant nothing, I did all this for nothing?'; 'Did it all mean nothing and was it all for nothing?'* She knows that it is all so meaningless and yet so meaningful. She can give herself the love she was much starved of. She can give herself the hug she so needed at that point of realisation. Only love is real. The only answer is love and love is the only answer. Everything else that is an illusion will fall away. She knows now where she comes from and that these apparent confines of her mind, her space, her physical space, are only a very funny and a very persistent illusion.

Lets feel more, lets open ourselves up for love, for nature for the divine soul that resides inside us all. In comparison with the sky we are all so small; but all so beautiful. It is this contrast we want to experience. How can we appear so tiny in proportion to a huge magnificent Universe and yet the Universe is us all?

See it expand in your head, in your mind's eye. When all false perception falls away you will become the stars. You will travel the stars. You will feel everyone you love and you have always loved in your bones and you will thank them for the role they played for you, and for all the teachings. Because they are you and you are them. You are the unlimited, the unbounded, the great potential of infinite creation. You are never alone, sometimes you just need to ask and remind yourself of that.

Feel it in your heart. So how can you be afraid of ascension? Afraid of the death of the ego? When it is just a falling away of wrong perception. It is the moment when a child realises he or she has just been tricked, that there is no monster under the bed or that the cookie only appears to be missing; and giggles in anticipation. You can cry as much as you want and release all you need if you feel you have to, but the point of action is to turn around. In turning around you see the beauty that is surrounding you constantly and renounce the false perception of fear. Walk the water if you have to, test us as much as you want, laugh, enjoy and breathe in the journey, but remember it is all temporary. Like a holiday at the water-park or a very persistent movie. Make it as beautiful as the sky that surrounds you, and let the sun remind you of home. The moon reminds you of your story to connect with your true self, your true purpose. Remember why you are here and why you chose to play all these different personas in different places. You can go home whenever you wish; home is a shift in perception.

Chapter 18- Lets break all the rules and then some

Let's break all the rules and then some! I am not suggesting anarchy here; I am just suggesting we start ridding ourselves of those very persistent, negative, automatic thoughts that pop up even when everything is going well. It's surprisingly easy to forget the good times when one is having a bad time. I keep trying to reach out and connect with people but all I get are vague answers which make me feel even more disconnected. I have my YouTube open on spiritual videos while I am trying to apply for jobs in Australia. The Australian Psychological Society has many forms to fill out which is making my head spin. Which way to go?

At the same time, yesterday I was in the park and I had a surprisingly nice day. Just hanging out with some lovely people without any fear, expectations or anything else ego-like which would cloud judgment. I forgot about what I had to do, to get to or what my ego wanted. Until today, when these demands came back so strongly and I started doubting myself so much it was paralysing. I had to sit on the rug and for ten minutes. I'd take a deep breath and say: '*I release X, Y and Z.*'

I spent some time releasing my need to control, my fear, my anxiety, my jealousy and all the ego traps while making room in my heart for the new. The energies were so intense that I don't even remember whether I posted the letter or not, what I had in my bag, and what I was supposed to do. While I get ready for yet another round of client-work I don't feel particularly excited about, I remember what it was like to be a kid and think that my dream life was somehow more real and exciting than my waking life. I need to switch things around again.

I am on my way for a wheatgrass juice and to offer some counselling. I feel ungrounded; I feel that the good times were somehow a deception. I remember the hard times and feel grateful before thinking to myself: *'Can it get any worse?'* and accidentally banging my head against the metal aircon boiler! I guess the answer is yes, it can always get worse. Let me realign with the better, with the magic and with hope and possibility. I don't even know anymore. I am about to speak to a lady who's just been raped and somehow the joys of helping people through the old models deceive me. I need to be out in a field with nature, reminded of the love that surrounds me. It's a little harder to connect to the heart chakra in the midst of a dense concrete jungle. I hope you follow me. This little paragraph is about the difficulty in showing the contrast between flow and resistance. What am I resisting right now? What are you resisting right now? Let's just let it go together.

'Remember what bliss feels like and the edges will feel much less sharp'. This is what Charis Melina Brown told me. You are creating and manifesting a painful experience as much as you created the joyful one. Although, sometimes this is easy to forget if you are not paying attention.

'Everything you take for granted is a blessing. Everything you fear is a friend in disguise. Everything you want is a part of you. Everything you hate you hate about yourself. Everything you own does not define you. Everything you feel is the only Truth there is to know.

Everything you wish for is already on its way to you. Everything you think creates your life. Everything you seek for you will find. Everything you resist will stick around. Everything you let go of stays if it's supposed to. Everything you need is right where you are.

Every time you bless another your bless yourself. Every time you blame another you lose your power. Every time you think you can, you can. Every time you fall you must get up and try again. Every time you cry you're one tear closer to joy. Every time you ask for forgiveness, all you have to do is forgive yourself.

Everyone you see is your reflection. Everyone you know mirrors you. Everyone wants to be happy. Everyone wants to live in joy. Everyone seeks a higher purpose. Everyone breathes the same breath. Everyone needs love to survive. Everyone has a purpose to fulfill.

Everyone's the same as everyone else. We just get caught up in labels, names, skin color and religion. Everyone's the same as everyone else. No one wants to feel the pain. Everyone's the same as everyone else. Everyone is dying for love to remain."

- **Jackson Kiddard**, author and polymath. (Taken from The Daily Love newsletter.)

This e-book is for my future children, whether they manifest a year from now or five years from now. It is an attempt to bridge the gap between spirituality and psychology. It is an attempt to light a spark within you to follow your bliss and to follow your heart.

Chapter 19- Into the eternal void we go

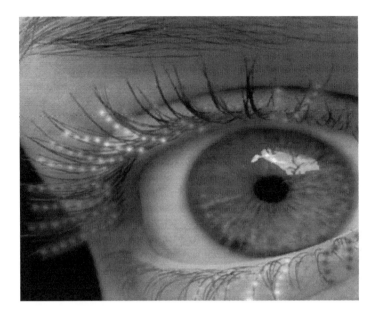

This is it. The book is getting too long and I might need to start writing the second book already. To conclude, the idea for this book was a calling and this is a work of love. I might lose a lot of friends by coming out of the spiritual closet and by stating clearly that my purpose is to help human beings in our evolutionary journey on Earth. To aim for ascension, love and unity consciousness. Some people, especially family, I foresee might argue, think I lost my marbles and disagree. Or this may further deepen our bond as I stand fast in my authenticity.

All I ask is that, even if you don't accept this, please respect my opinion. If you are still my friend then I love you much more for standing alongside me through all of it.

If you are a new friend then I am ever so grateful to be connecting with this new energy and people on a similar level of consciousness, which is why I wrote this book. There is no point in hiding who you are anymore to be 'accepted.' There is no point in fear and doubt and thinking you will be rejected if you share the most intimate parts of your soul. This is the age of the new dawn, so be bold, be brave, take risks, be strong and stop numbing your emotions. Spiritual teachers and psychologists will tell you emotions are key. Stop consuming fear, eating fear, watching fear and then wondering why you are afraid. Watch your thoughts and if you feel like you don't belong, never feel at home and are often sad, I say let's embrace this together! I used to look into mirrors wondering who the hell I was. I thought that by learning about psychology and fixing others I could fix me. But no one could have told me anything I didn't already know.

Who will you be when it all falls away?

All the answers you seek are inside you, it is just an awakening of knowledge... but how can you access this knowledge if you are afraid of being alone? Who are you in those empty moments? You are the eternal I AM presence.

It was when I met Viet, that I felt I needed to access my loneliness. Normally I would have tried to run away from this

Only your ego is afraid of what may come next.

The ego is not real, I know you will resist this at first but your name, your social identity, your material possessions, your achievements and all you are doing will fall away. None of that stuff will bring you happiness. It sounds cliché but people often forget and get mistaken. Your worth is inherent and not dependent on any of these things. You may feel sad when you read this if you haven't accessed this part of yourself yet. True life only appears to be limited because we see death as the ultimate limitation. It is when I felt extremely alone after coming back from a holiday that I felt I needed to meditate to really access this emptiness. Normally I would have tried to run away from it. Instead, I felt much better by accepting that I was lonely but not alone; I healed my soul of this seeking.

Once you heal the spiritual and emotional hunger, the physical hunger tends to go away as well. Don't even get me started on diet and lifestyle as other people know more about this than me at this stage. Do your own research. Raw vegan works for me as it makes my eyes brighter and my head clearer, but I hear it is not for everybody. Listen to your body. When I started meditating every day I could no longer ignore the voice that reminded me that I was *'tucking into a dead animal'* when eating a piece of salmon. I am learning to honour my feelings and so I do not enjoy *'tucking into dead animals'* any longer. I am integrating, transforming, transmuting, transitioning and this is part of my integration.

I am not going to get burned at the stake for speaking my truth. Criticism is ok when I know my core being and my truth. It is all a myriad of different perspectives, there is no right or wrong but some things might feel right or wrong for you specifically.

The fear of loneliness still creeps up every once in a while. I felt alone on holiday even when I was surrounded by people. Sometimes you feel even more alone when you are surrounded but not seen. When I was growing up and someone would call me ugly in school I believed them because I didn't know who I was. I thought that by fixing my hair, buying the right clothes, working out, I would somehow be accepted and fit the mould. We all go through this growing up. I started shutting down. For instance, I started shutting down my connection with animals. This was difficult because, when I would bond with a lamb at my uncle's farm I had to realise they would sacrifice it and it felt so wrong to me at an energetic level. Yet, I shut it down. I shut down when I heard animals being killed, I shut down my sensitivity, I shut down my ability to see auras because I wanted to be cool at school. I shut down so much that if I had shut down for another year I would have been underground!

I coped with intellect and sarcasm. I laughed when people accidentally hurt themselves. It took a journey of psychology, academia, deep searching, then pain and realisation to get to where I needed to be; to get back to my authentic truth, my authentic self and reconnect with emotions.

I saw Nick Good recently speak about his superhero training in London. He told us about Ho'oponopono which is an ancient Hawaiian practice of reconciliation and forgiveness. We did this exercise where you connect with your heart and say: '*I am sorry, please forgive me, I love you. Thank you Thank you Thank you.*'

Do it now. Hold your hands against your heart and try it for a few minutes really trying to connect with the traumatized inner child most of us try to ignore and deny. I didn't think much of it at the time but I woke up in tears. My ego had started to show me all the ways in which I had shut it down and I started remembering things I hadn't thought about in years!

'A pearl is a beautiful thing that is produced by an injured life. It is the tear [that results] from the injury of the oyster. The treasure of our being in this world is also produced by an injured life. If we had not been wounded, if we had not been injured, then we will not produce the pearl.'

- **Stephan Hoeller**, writer, scholar and religious leader. (Quote from The Daily Love Newsletter.)

Therefore, nothing you can do to me, and nothing anyone can do to you will change who you are. I am purging my soul on these pages not because I am a narcissist but because it is only with truth that we can resonate. By resonating with this truth you can access your own truth as we are all One. We are all connected and we are all part of Source. We are the unlimited potential of creation and once you remember that why would you want to follow someone else's rules? Why would you look outside of yourself for how to be pretty, how to be magical, how to fit into a job that will sap away all your energy?

All I know is that when I climb up on the roof of my London flat sometimes and I look at the clouds, I am baffled by their beauty. Have you ever been knocked back when you look up at the starry skies? This is the feeling I am talking about, a feeling often drowned and forgotten in our day to day lives. A feeling of awe that is so raw, so real that it is hard to imagine for a moment what you need to do, where you need to go, who you are. Because everything is Perfect just the way it is. Because you are Perfect just the way you are, and I love you very much in your essence. Fear is useless and exhausting. *'The more of the Universe you take in, the more you understand about yourself because you are the Universe."* Jordan SpiritPatch.

Thank you and so long for now my friends. I know you will be successful and you will have fun in all that you do. Thank you for sticking with me this far and I hope you enjoyed this e-book. I hope parts of it resonate with deep aspects of your Being and your Soul and I hope that if not, at least you will have enjoyed the humorous bits. What is the point of taking life seriously anyway? Let's jump back on the rollercoaster once in a while on the way to total bliss. Although since parking the ego as much as possible, my rollercoaster has been a merry go round. Thank you to all my new magical friends who I send a lot of love to wherever you are.

This book has some typos and grammatical errors but I keep being told to get it out there and that it doesn't need to be perfect. This book maps out the territory and is an important part of my integration as it deals directly with fear in the face of death. Fear is something we can all relate to. Watch out for my next book with more finely tuned downloads.

Finally, my experience is not intended as a direct criticism of the NHS (they are doing their best I hope.) Thank you to all of those who pushed my ego buttons forcing me to evolve consciousness. We will only grow and evolve by shining the Light into those dark aspects of our personality we were told to hide by our society. How can you evolve unless you release all the emotional garbage you are carrying around? I assure you, freedom is bliss.

The songs: Bonobo *'Black Sands'* and *'Kiara';* Tiesto *'Empty Streets';* Kristin Luna Ray *'Sita Ram';* Adele *'Set Fire to the Rain';* and India Arie *'Nature'* have provided a nice soundtrack whilst writing this e-book.